Essays That Worked—
For Law Schools

Also by Boykin Curry (with Brian Kasbar)

Essays That Worked:
50 Essays from Successful Applications
to the Nation's Top Colleges

Essays That Worked—For Business Schools

Essays THAT WORKED

FOR LAW SCHOOLS

35 Essays from Successful Applications
to the Nation's Top Law Schools

Edited by Boykin Curry

Mustang Publishing
New Haven

Library of Congress Cataloging in Publication Data:

Essays that worked for law schools.

    1. Law schools--United States--Admission.   I. Curry, Boykin, 1966-
KF285.E87 1988   340'.07'1173   88-60509
ISBN 0-914457-24-1 (pbk.)

10 9 8 7 6 5 4 3 2 1

For Rollin Riggs,
a publisher and a friend,
who with patience, humor, hard work,
and entrepreneurial spirit gives life to ideas.

Acknowledgments

This book was derived from the efforts of many students and admissions officers at some of the top law schools in America. We deeply appreciate the generosity of the applicants who let us reprint their essays and of the admissions officers who gave us their time, critiques, and advice.

We wish to extend our gratitude to several people in particular: Debbie Land and Christina Benet, students at Yale who helped with the production of this book, and Jean Webb at the Yale Law School and Kent Frandsen at Indiana University at Indianapolis Law School. All went far beyond their duties and gave us invaluable assistance. Thank you very much.

Boykin Curry
August, 1988

Contents

Introduction

How important is the essay on a law school application?

Along with your grades, your accomplishments, and, in some cases, your LSAT scores, your application essay can determine whether you are accepted or rejected. For some law schools, the essay is crucial: a great essay can make admissions officers discount poor grades or scores; a bad essay can ruin an otherwise sterling application. For other schools, the essay is considered seriously only on borderline candidates and is used only to "tip the scales."

It all depends on the school. One admissions officer told us flatly, "We do not use the essay as a major factor." Another officer said, "The essay is not going to vault someone to the top of the pack from the middle, but it can be determinative for some middle-of-the-road applicants. And it is more important than that for minority applicants."

Said still another: "It is a vital element of our admissions policy."

After speaking with admissions officers at a variety of law schools, we tried to estimate just how important the essay can be in the admissions process. The following graph illustrates roughly the relative importance of the essay at these schools:

	Irrelevant		**Vital**
	0	5	10
Harvard	▬▬▬▬▬▬▬▬▬▬▬▬▬▬▬▬▬▬		
Columbia	▬▬▬▬▬▬▬▬▬▬▬▬▬		
Yale	▬▬▬▬▬▬▬▬▬▬▬▬▬▬▬▬▬▬		

	Irrelevant		Vital
	0	5	10

Duke

New York U.

U. Michigan

Berkeley

UCLA

UNC/Chapel Hill

U. Washington

Tulane

Northeastern

Boston Univ.

U. Iowa

Northwestern

Indiana

Florida State

Stanford

U. Penn

U. Chicago

Cornell

In our previous books on college and business school application essays, we discussed what kinds of content and tone were most appropriate. Much of our earlier advice holds true for law school applications as well.

Overwhelmingly, admissions officers everywhere complain about the same thing: reading 13,000 essays on the same few topics in just three months is a mind-numbing experience. Most essays are dry and over-written. They are often "corrected" by so many friends and relatives that the life gets sucked out. One undergraduate admissions officer noted that "few applicants understand what we want to read, and they rarely go out on a limb to be witty or controversial." Anxious applicants become so afraid of saying the wrong thing that they say nothing at all. Such sterilization can mean unbearable monotony for the hapless reader, so don't treat your essay like a psychological minefield. What seems "safe" to you may be deadly boring to a weary admissions officer.

The officer at one top business school resorted to dramatic measures to combat essay fatigue. "I try to change the scenery when I read essays," he said. "I read them in the park or out on my boat. You know what? Even that doesn't help."

Now imagine that same cynical admissions officer finding your live-ly, original essay in the middle of the pile. For starters, your application is *noticed*—and most likely remembered—and that is much of the bat-tle. Plus, you have done a favor for the tired reader. Favors are often returned.

"I've noticed that law faculty who are on admissions committees typical-ly want to know why the candidate wants to go to law school," one Dean of Admissions said wearily. "I don't much care about that. I just want an essay that grabs me."

A piece doesn't have to be a hilarious comedy or a literary jewel to "grab" the reader. Something which is simple, honest, and sincere can be more disarming than sophisticated humor or strategic pledges to work for worldwide justice.

The buzzword among admissions officers these days is "authenticity," but it describes what admissions officers will always want: some kind of proof that you are a lively, sensitive, bright person with whom they can *identify*.

After reading the essays in this book, we hope you will understand better the boundaries of tone and content within which you can work, and we hope you see how large those boundaries are. Some of the essays are written masterfully. Some are a little clumsy, and some are, frankly, rather dull. But, in the opinion of the admissions officer who sent it to us, each essay "worked." Why? Because it revealed a part of the applicant's personality that wasn't shown in grades and LSAT scores. Each writer took the opportunity to convert a large chunk of fearsome blank paper into a personal message to the admissions staff. And that's the whole point of the exercise.

Since these essays represent some of the best out of thousands submitted each year, they should serve to inspire your creativity and help you feel more comfortable about the admissions process. As the essays demonstrate, you can be exciting and natural without resorting to outrageous gimmicks or immature poses. And you don't have to be Ernest Hemingway—or even an English major—to write an effective personal statement. An honest, enthusiastic reflection of your personality can make for a refreshing—and we hope successful—essay. Good luck!

An Interview
With An Admissions Officer

Although different schools attach different levels of importance to the application essays, and although each school may be looking for a slightly different type of student, admissions officers have surprisingly similar desires. They want brevity. They want sincerity. They want mature enthusiasm. And a little humor—when it's truly humorous—doesn't hurt.

But as we pondered the application question and tried to compose our own "Personal Statement," we found ourselves asking a number of questions. How "lawyer-like" should we be? How much can we joke around? Can we relax and be the readers' chum, or should we treat them as clients? Should we tell them what we think they want to hear, or should we be totally honest, even at the risk of being dull?

We asked these and other questions to dozens of admissions officers at almost every major law school in the country. The following is a condensed version of those interviews, along with relevant comments from admissions people whom we interviewed earlier at business schools and colleges:

What's the difference between application essays for law school and the essays we wrote to get into college?
The main difference is the way the author presents himself. What we ask of a college graduate is much more difficult than what colleges ask of a high-school senior. And it should be. We don't want applicants to simply give a self-absorbed description of themselves, like they did for their college application. Rather, we want them to describe the world they see around them, and their place in it. An analogy we like to use around here is that with the essay, a student fashions a lens for us to

view the world. From looking at the quality of that lens, we hope to judge the quality of its maker.

We also expect more maturity for law school. That's partly a function of age but it's also an issue of direction. Undergraduates are coming to school to explore. It's hard to justify giving one of a few spots to someone who is not pretty committed to a law career.

I used your undergraduate book for a talk I gave on the application essay, but I had to warn everyone that this is not high school any more. Some of the essays in your first book would have been fine, but others are way too cutesy for us. Essays about socks and pets and Oreos [essays that "worked" for colleges] would be a real detriment to a law school application.

Do you want a description of a person or just a prose listing of accomplishments?
We want an essay that brings the whole set of numbers into a coherent form. We want inconsistencies explained, and we want to see diverse activities as different facets of a single personality. We'd like to be able to say, "Oh, he did that, yeah, that makes sense. That fits with what we have." Both the performer and his track record should be discussed, so that we can know the person underneath all the accomplishments, and also how those activities affected that person.

Nine times out of ten, people who write a really good personal statement don't have the supporting facts to back it up. A student will say he wants to be a lawyer to stop racial injustice, but then he'll write an essay about "learning to scuba dive helped me overcome my fear of water" or something. Tell me about your legal aid work, or your work in the Big Brother program, or something like that. Inconsistency knocks an applicant down quite a few pegs in my judgement.

Are there any hackneyed topics that applicants should avoid?
'Why I want to be a public defender...' or 'I have always wanted to be a lawyer since I was ten. My daddy was a lawyer and he took me to court and I enjoyed it...' I mean, who cares? Do they really expect us to think some kind of immaculate revelation hit them at age ten? It makes me wonder if they have thought carefully about the decision they are making.

It may sound insensitive, but a common essay which almost never works is about 'my mother's death' or 'my medical history.' They're almost always manipulative, and they rarely come to important conclusions.

If such an incident truly reveals your character, fine, but we're looking for much more than just another hard-luck story.

'What I think about justice' is also far too common. Since we are a law school, of course, I suppose it's to be expected, but so many people do it that you have to write a very good essay to stand out. Also, since we know the law and the students have not yet studied it, essays on the law risk sounding naive and ill-informed. I'm not saying an applicant should avoid this topic; just don't jump straight to it.

Of course, then someone starts up, 'Since I was ten...' and bursts into something truly wonderful. Really, the similarity in topics is not what makes essays dull—and most of them certainly are. It's the monotonous style. Applicants tend to use too many big words and amorphous adjectives and not enough colorful details and observations.

The first 50 essays that come in are okay, but by 3,575 we start to look at them very quickly—and they'd better have something interesting to say.

If reading essays is so boring, would you prefer that applicants try to entertain you?
It's not their job to do that, and the applicants who are accepted tend not to have massive entertainment value. We also read no more than 20 essays at a sitting, so that shock value doesn't take on overriding importance. Still, I do confess to some weakness for catchy or clever turns.

Nothing is worse than something that seems unnatural, though—and gimmicks do not work. One year we got an essay written in crayon on construction paper. It really hurt the applicant because it made us question his maturity and competence. That kind of joking might work occasionally for a college application, but we are dealing with much more sophisticated people at this level. Jokers are admitted only if their credentials are so good that we just can't refuse them.

You do have to captivate the reader somewhat, but many people hurt themselves by going too far. One applicant wrote an eight-page essay when we asked for one page. She was entertaining, but she didn't arrive at any point. And she didn't get very far in the admissions process, either.

Being off-beat just to get attention won't work. The uniqueness has to mesh with the rest of the application. We do want to see different facets of an applicant's personality. We do want people to show us how they differ from the other 7,000 applicants. But different doesn't mean outrageous. It can mean a paralegal who takes ghetto kids camping on weekends, or a math major with a passion for billiards. It does not mean some goofball just trying to impress us with a bunch of one-liners.

Some applicants have sent videotapes and put ads in the newspaper here. Unless it shows some relevant skill in a very meaningful way, a display like that is a waste of time.

I suppose my best advice is to write a mature essay—nothing too formal, though—and to integrate your personality into it as best you can. Don't be afraid to say what you feel. Remember that serious is not synonymous with humorless. We love wit, but it also has to be backed up with meaningful points.

Is motivation important? Do you want to see what an applicant plans to do with the degree?
Motivation can be important, but it must be explained and supported. Everyone talks about wanting to help people. Why? What motivates you, specifically?

From what I read, you would think everyone is going into *pro bono* work as soon as they graduate. Of course, we know that won't happen. We are sensitive to the fact that many essays may be contrived to what the applicant thinks are the committee's priorities. Since an undergraduate has no real notion of all the options available in the legal profession, an essay about "here's the kind of law I plan to be practicing in 20 years" is really not very valuable.

Do you want a good writer or a good person?
Both, of course. A vote on that might divide our committee 3-3, but I think writing quality may edge-out the limited insight we can glean from a 300-word essay. Expressing yourself is a key part of the profession, after all. You may never have to argue a case in court, but you'll always have to write. We want to know about you, but behind that is whether you can deal with the language and communicate.

Good writers are convincing and engaging. They know how to intrigue an audience, and they back up their points with specific, relevant details. Their ideas flow smoothly, and they make the reader's job a lot easier. And if they are intelligent and witty, the essay is hard to forget.

One applicant wrote an essay wondering why people on death row always ask for a cigarette instead of writing down something about their lives or even making a last statement. Well, it is incredibly hard to express yourself, and we know that, so don't let your anxiety about style interfere with your need to write a meaningful essay.

There'd better be no typos, though—it's amazing how many we get. We are always getting letters two weeks after receiving an essay apologizing for mistakes. Lots of times they enclose a "revised copy." Well, if they care so much about getting into our law school, why didn't they read over the essay before they sent it? I don't want to be distracted by grammar mistakes and organizational problems. There is no excuse for not having your essay reviewed by friends or a teacher. It should be polished.

The essay isn't the only view we get of your articulation skills. We get writing on your LSAT writing sample, too. The essay shows us what an applicant can do in a longer period of time, of course, but sometimes we wonder if the essay and the writing sample could possibly have been written by the same person.

So what are you looking for?
Truthfully, we don't have a set agenda. We don't know what we're looking for until we read it.

I want to know who the applicant is and why she wants to go to law school. How she thinks. Or what she cares about. Sometimes I've been in tears by the end of an essay. Occasionally one will make me laugh for the rest of the day. But most successful essays need not be dramatic. We want people to be vibrant, but we don't want gimmicks. We want a mature approach, but we don't want to be fed dull, pompous lines.

I want an honest, thoughtful essay. I know that sounds a little trite, but it's something we rarely see. Not only is that the best essay to read, but it should be the easiest to write. Concocting ridiculous anecdotes, attention-getting schemes, or a fictitious portrait is really a big waste of time and energy.

Everyone wants us to give a recipe and a roadmap to the admissions process, but what we want is someone who can navigate his own course. Within guidelines, of course.

The Basic Essay Question

The following essay question was found on a recent application to an Ivy League law school. While the topic on applications varies somewhat, this is basically what you can expect:

You may wish to submit a statement or essay supplementing required application materials, which would provide the Admissions Committee with information regarding such matters as personal, family or educational background, experiences and talents of special interest, one's reason for applying to law school as they may relate to personal goals and professional expectations, or any other factors which you think should inform the Committee's evaluation of your candidacy for admission. Such a statement should be submitted with the application materials.

The Essays

For organizational purposes, we have divided the essays into eight groups. We created the introductions to each group based on our own research and on comments submitted by admissions officers when they sent us the essays. Please understand that this grouping is totally artificial. You don't have to write an essay that would fit neatly into one of these categories.

As well as being a fine piece of writing, an essay might also exemplify a "type." For example, the piece on the death of Michael Stewart (page 87) is a good example of an essay on injustice, a common theme. So, if you are going to write this type of essay, pay close attention to the advice in the group's introduction, as well as to the actual essays.

The essays that follow are reproduced exactly as they were submitted, though of course the typeface and spacing are different. We did not correct punctuation, spelling, or grammatical errors in the essays. But note that rarely would such correction be necessary.

Since the authors of some essays requested anonymity, we sometimes have deleted proper names and substituted a more general name in place of a specific reference. In addition, at the request of a few schools, we sometimes disguised the name of the school to which the writer applied. However, our substitutions never distort the content of the essay.

Finally, a warning. Though we know that no one would be foolish enough to copy these essays verbatim, we also know that some readers might be tempted to take an essay and "change it around" to suit their applications. We hope you realize how incredibly stupid that would be. For one thing, stealing an idea from an essay in this book or "paraphrasing" it would be dishonest—and maybe even a criminal violation of copyright. For another thing, it would severely jeopardize your chance of getting into a law school. Most admissions officers have read this book, and none would ever admit a plagiarist.

The following pages demonstrate the creative potential of the law school application essay. We hope these essays will inspire you when you begin to write, and we hope they will give you the confidence to write a bold, personal piece that will show an admissions committee why you are special. Enjoy the essays, study them, and let them be a catalyst for your own creativity.

Pyro-Imagery Overload

A law school admissions officer noted that he could expect one metaphor in almost every essay. Before you decide to carry a torch for the same image, allow this flash to scald your mind: fire imagery is trite. Take our advice and don't get burned. No matter how incendiary your essay may be, extinguish the pyrotechnics. The lines below were taken from actual essays:

"My involvement with music sparked a passion..."
"My mind blazed with the possibilities..."
"My interest in law was kindled at an early age..."
"My passion was ignited from the day..."
"The memory of that injustice burnt within me..."

To Have What It Takes:
Essays About Character

Law school—and the profession in general—is demanding. No admissions officer wants to admit students who were glitzed by *LA Law*. Law school means spending hours through the night pouring over obscure cases written in some of the most colorless prose since your tenth-grade algebra text. It is not glamorous. It is rarely fun. It takes hard work, self-discipline, and a high tolerance for boredom and exhaustion to become a great lawyer.

If you have endured before, and done so with humor and good nature, by all means tell your story. Don't be a martyr, though. Whining complaints about all your hardships are tiresome. The reader will think: If it's so bad, why doesn't he persue something less demanding? Miserable students—even hard-working, miserable students—bring down everyone else. No professor wants a classroom full of bright but depressed legal minds.

High spirits, on the other hand, are infectious. In Thomas Kelly's essay, the playful tone makes you think he really *enjoys* living in the squalor of the West African bush. If he can laugh about his fly-infested food and the battle to acquire it, a long night of study or a stressful trial will be a cakewalk to him.

The writer of the next essay does a good job of turning the problems she faced (some of which appeared on her transcript) into a story of personal victory. By itself, a low grade in sophomore French might have hurt her application, but accompanied by this essay, the lapse is likely to be overlooked.

The last essay uses a list form to make its points. Such a format (not to mention the sexist title) is unlikely to charm many admissions officers, but a list is a good way to make your points without a lot of distracting verbiage.

Thomas A. Kelly, III

For two years I have been a Peace Corps volunteer in the Republic of Niger in West Africa. I live in a grass hut in a tiny village called Fandou-Berri, sixty-five kilometers from the nearest city. I subsist primarily on a diet of rice, millet paste and leaf sauce. Once a week I travel twenty kilometers to the village of Hamdallaye where I can buy goat meat. Each time I walk away from the Hamdallaye market, having bargained for a fair chunk of meat, I think of Mrs. H., an attorney at Paul, Hastings, Janofsky and Walker in Washington, D.C. She was known in the office as the Velvet Steamroller. It was said that she could bargain the shirt off of your back and make you believe that you had gotten the better of the deal. When I was a paralegal, I admired her technique. Now I wish she could see me deal with the butchers in Hamdallaye.

Because there are no scales in the West African bush, meat is sold by the pile. Normally, an amount of money is stated in advance, then the size of the pile is haggled over. When buying meat in Hamdallaye the size of the pile depends on a confluence of factors. Is the butcher working alone, or does he have to demonstrate his business acumen to his fellow butchers by slighting the foreigner? Is he in a good or even charitable mood? This will determine whether he will follow the practice of throwing one last large chunk on the pile after the bargain has been struck—the butcher's version of the baker's dozen. I have learned to judge the butcher's expressions as I approach the meat section of the market, then isolate a sympathetic looking one.

Is the buyer in the mood to haggle? This can work two ways. Some days the best strategy is to stare expressionlessly at the pile as it mounts, guilting the butcher into being fair. Other days, particularly if there is a crowd for the butcher to play to, one must haggle aggressively for the entire second half of the pile. If the buyer's approach does not correspond to the butcher's mood and to the prevailing conditions, he is certain to come away the loser.

The object itself often looks decidedly not worth the argument. The various body parts, including gaping eyeballs and oozing entrails lie on the table intermixed with the choice cuts of meat. There is no Styrofoam to mask the reality of what happened to that goat just minutes before. So many flies swarm on the meat that the haggling must be done in a raised voice so that both parties can hear over the buzzing.

The butcher closes the deal by reaching for his equivalent of wax paper—a U.S.A.I.D. cement sack. He tears off a piece, smacks it, which sends a cloud of cement dust into the air, then wraps up the portion of goat meat for transport. The transaction is complete.

If there is, in the curriculum of the law school I attend, a course in bargaining, perhaps Mrs. H. and I can teach it together.

(Name Withheld)

When I was ten years old, I had a feisty pony named Merrylegs. Every once in awhile, as I teetered on her narrow backbone, she would get this wild look in her eye just before bolting
off down the road. All I could do was hang on and pray that I
wouldn't fall off and die like this guy on "Bonanza". I managed
to hold my ground (although sometimes I ended up there) for
about five years, and then my legs sprouted down so that when
I sat atop Merrylegs, if I rocked from side to side, I could feel
the precious earth beneath my feet.

As a teenager, my legs were long and skinny—the perfect
legs for a cross-country runner. All through high school I per-
formed on the track and cross-country teams, running the two
mile race with my dad on the sidelines keeping my splits on his
Timex wristwatch. I was no champion runner. I don't remember ever breaking the tape to the wild applause of the fans. But
I remember making it across the finish line every time—
sometimes grimacing, sometimes smiling—never giving up.

College was another test of perseverance. As I watched my
parents drive away in their stationwagon, the dust from Minnesota thick on the back window, I started to cry. I didn't
know a soul on this sprawling Big Ten campus. And what did I
know about Iowa, except that between each endless cornfield
there was a pig farm.

Desperate for company, I went to church with a girl from my
dorm. When the kneeling bench was pulled out, I thought it
was a footstool. I knew the Presbyterians didn't allow such
comfort during church services, but these Episcopalians were
all right. A perplexed glance from my dormmate was all I
needed to quickly slide my feet to the floor. I spent prayer time
ruminating about the congregation—they didn't all look like
pig farmers to me. Maybe there was more to Iowa than I
thought. There definitely was more to religion than I thought.

Keen on acquiring new information, I prowled the campus. Why are you guys wearing arm bands? Because John Lennon's been shot. Who's John Lennon? You kiddin' me? He's one of the Beatles. Who're the Beatles? Whoa! You don't know who the *Beatles* are? Let me tell you a thing or two about music . . . and politics . . . and how to conjugate French verbs . . .

By second semester, sophomore year, I was waiting for my second wind. I was losing ground on my studies and losing sight of French altogether. Balancing academics and a social life was like teetering on a narrow backbone, and one night, determined to bale out of both, I hiked to the Greyhound Bus station.

I didn't board the bus, and graduated two years later. I knew that whatever challenges I had to face—grueling workouts, suicidal horseback rides, college—I could face them and I could learn from them. Even if I wasn't the top horsewoman or runner or English major, I was someone who would hang in there and see something through to the end. My most significant accomplishment has been to persevere.

(Name Withheld)

I am an extremely goal-oriented individual. Self-motivation has been an important impetus in my life. For example, as a high school senior, I set one financial goal for the next four years. I would pay all collegiate expenses without parental or governmental aid. Perhaps this was a bit zealous for an 18 year-old with only a token summer job. I decided that attending a regional campus for two years while working 15 to 35 hours per week would best help me recognize my goal. Frugality prevailed during this time. Now, as a college senior, I realize my goal may have been somewhat unrealistic, but I have paid for 80 percent of those expenses.

Second, I am a very organized person. During my freshman year of college, I implemented a system of budgeting my time. Each night, I began to allot the following day's time in half-hour increments. It is a practice I still maintain.

Third, I am a leader. Two roles I have played are important in this assessment. At age 19, I was selected to be foreman of a jury trying a criminal case in my hometown. I was by far the youngest of the jurors and was actively involved in every part of the deliberation, seeking out each juror's opinion on points made in discussion.

Lastly, being very personable, I feel, is one of my stronger attributes. My work experience provides the one best example of this. As a sales representative for a construction corporation the previous two summers in my hometown, I was responsible for meeting with five to eight customers per day in a dyad setting. Because in our market there existed no differential advantages between competitors, my job entailed getting the customer to believe in me so he would then believe in the company I represented. I had the highest sales-close percentage in the firm.

Several activities fill my free time. As a member of Beta

Alpha Psi, the national honorary accounting society, I am currently involved with the Alumni Committee. We are working on a project to keep alumni informed of chapter events and, hopefully, we will deliver a newsletter to them in mid-December.

Sports have always provided me with great enjoyment. It was because of my love of children and basketball that I spent two years as head coach of a fourth-grade YMCA basketball team. It was one of the most fulfilling activities of my life.

Culturally, I am also intent upon expanding myself. I am captivated by the study of history, especially European political history as it pertains to the two world wars. I also have a keen interest in politics and, time permitting, will work in the upcoming election.

My greatest academic achievement, though, is that I have received a very intensive education in accounting along with a very broad diversion into many other academic fields. This education has rounded my individual being and, consequently, I am not just a business major.

My aspirations are to practice law in a business environment. I am enthralled by how law applies to business and the effects of the business community upon the formation of the law.

I will be successful in law school because my undergraduate work has prepared me. As I understand, four skills are necessary for an undergraduate to develop if he desires to do well in law.

First, developed communication skills are imperative. To accomplish this objective, I planned a cirriculum that emphasized essay exams, term papers, classroom participation, and oral presentations. Fifteen hours of history, nine of political science, six of English, and three each of communication, philosophy, sociology, and psychology have I taken. My cumulative G.P.A. in the above 42 hours of coursework is 3.86.

Second, the above courses were also beneficial to me not in how they were taught but in what they taught. An understanding of society and its problems is an important asset for a prospective law student. The above courses are one avenue to a greater understanding of society and the role of law within society.

Third, many legal questions focus upon a business consideration. Thus, the prepared law student has an understanding of the business community and the implications of the law upon it. My coursework in finance, economics, marketing, operations, and accounting (my major) has provided me this knowledge. My cumulative G.P.A. in accounting is 3.66.

Lastly, logical thought processes are an important instrument for the undergraduate to possess. I have developed my analytical tools in nine hours of mathematics, six hours of science, and three hours of philosophy. My cumulative G.P.A. in the above courses is 3.5.

In conclusion, I must comment upon the wide disparity in my two LSAT sittings. During the month preceding the first sitting, I was experiencing some personal problems. I had not resolved them by test date and I feel they impacted negatively upon my performance. I resolved them shortly afterwards. For this reason, I feel my second score is more indicative of my abilities and I would ask you give that score greater weight when evaluating my potential.

The Ideal Man

—25 to 35; college and preferably MBA degree

—a man of poise and stature with instant and favorable impact at high executive levels

—alert, quick, able to think on his feet and decide whether to fight, fence or withdraw

—objective, thorough and penetrating in analysis with a strong sense of logic; dealing at the facts level, rather than subjective level

—imaginative and resourceful in developing original solutions to management problems; able to communicate with and motivate top management by talking with, not at, them

—ambitious, energetic and persistent; able to take ups and downs and never give up

—able to deal with project type work; have several balls in the air and still get work done

—"result conscious," accomplishment motivated and "first things first" person

—a team worker; responsive and understanding in dealing with others; able to command respect at all levels

—skillful in oral and written expression; able to sell his ideas

—intensely interested in people, their actions, reactions and motivations; able to establish emphatic rapport quickly; listen carefully and analyze objectively

—able to identify and assess climate, direction, aims, opportunities and problems of a corporation from an overall "chief executive level" viewpoint rather than concentrate on its specific functional areas

Be True To Your School:
Essays About Why You
and the School Are Well-Matched

An admissions officer sent us an essay she liked, and she included a personal note. "The fact that this essay is tailored to our school and mentions me by name," read part of her letter, "is unimportant and unnecessary."

Maybe.

Any indication that you have looked carefully at the schools you want to attend can make you seem more mature. You want to persuade the admissions officer that you would be a good fit with the school. But be careful. Don't spoil your observations with effusive language and gratuitous praise.

"We get a lot of applicants writing, 'Your school has an internationally renowned reputation,'" one admissions officer said, "and you know they wrote the same thing to 12 other schools."

Even if you honestly believe that a school has "an exciting and diverse student body, brilliant professors, and an excellent program of study," telling them this says nothing about you.

Every law school has some fine aspects, and a candidate who has researched the school can speak to them. Doing so could convince the admissions officer to let you in—or reject you. If you cannot substantiate your argument that you "fit" the school well, the fit will be contrived, and the admissions officer will spot it a mile away.

Yale Law School is known for its politically active, often left-wing students and faculty, and an essay about your compassion for the oppressed might be well-received there. But if your history of activism consists of ringing doorbells for Ronald Reagan one weekend in 1984, you're not going to need directions to New Haven.

The law schools at the University of Chicago and the University of Michigan are regarded as rather traditional, where hard work may count for more than political activism. Telling Dean Smith in Ann Arbor that you are "inspired by the demanding workload at Michigan" will fall flat if your grades are mediocre.

So consider a wide range of law schools, and if you do see a match, then by all means exploit it. But don't try to play on the admissions officers egos or stupidity. They've seen it all before—many, many times.

Jean Skelton Fraser

My grandfather, dean of the Minnesota Law School and
alumnus of Harvard Law, had one thing to say about Yale Law
School. "If you want to learn sociology," he said, "go to Yale. If
you want to learn law, go somewhere else."

Though my grandfather may turn over in his grave, Yale is
my first choice. As my parents have shown, an understanding
of our legal system is of great value in effecting social change.
I believe that my father's legal training has made him a more
responsible and effective congressman and mayor. For example,
he vetoed an anti-pornography ordinance whose goals he agreed
with because it infringed upon the right to free speech. My
mother, who has worked in and out of government, also
stresses the importance of change within the context of exist-
ing institutions. Having been caught in Uganda in the recent
coup, she is only too aware of the fragility of our defenses
against rule by violence.

Only fair law justly applied keeps us from anarchy. Law is
the expression of a complex interaction between our cultural
values and the structure of our society. Because I want to
change the attitudes and the structure, I need to understand
our legal system, not just the law codes. What fascinates me is
the process as well as the end product. At Yale I want to learn
how our laws have been developed and applied in the past to be
more effective at changing them in the future.

(Name Withheld)

As an undergraduate student at The University of Iowa, I recall the campus was always changing. I saw the Communications Center go up, I saw the Old Armory come down. The changes were not only external, but internal as well: information systems were updated, fields of study were expanded. The U of I looked for opportunities to improve and then dug right in.

This summer I dug right in when I realized I had an interest in law. Researching Iowa's Law School Program, I came across the literature on the Joint Program and was impressed by how perceptive Iowa was of my needs. Of course the Joint Program wasn't designed just for me, I remind myself, but nevertheless, I am excited by the similar view I share with Iowa: to develop a broad perspective.

The University of Iowa is always striving to be better. So am I. Law school is my opportunity for challenge and change. If I am fortunate enough to get accepted into the U of I Law Program or the Joint Program, I will enroll with energy and enthusiasm. I can't think of a better place to broaden my perspectives—and hopefully someday practice law—than Iowa, my Heartland.

Excuses, Excuses:
Essays That Explain an Aberration

An essay that admissions people see often—too often—is the one about "why I did poorly on the LSAT" or "I am an over-achiever even though my grades don't show it." What may seem like a legitimate explanation to you usually comes across as a whiny excuse for poor performance to the reader.

"Apologizing," said one officer, "is invariably uninformative. If you were so active in extra-curriculars that you couldn't study, we will see that elsewhere on the application. And telling us that you are a 'bad tester' is just a throwaway. We know the LSATS aren't perfect, and we factor that in. But what are applicants expecting when they write, 'I really am quite intelligent; I just test poorly'? That we will knock their score up a few points to compensate? I mean, if they wanted to waste the space, every applicant with a score from 12 to 47 could say that they are 'smarter than the test indicates'."

Generally, the personal statement is the wrong place to apologize. There are so many important things to discuss about yourself that to squander the small space—or even a part of it—shortchanges your own story and irritates admissions people.

If you do have some objective and new explanation for an aberration in grades, LSATS, or discipline record, some officers suggested that you attach an addendum to your application. "An apology is always superfluous, but if you have a real justification for some lapse, then by all means write it down and send it in. If you don't mention it, then I guarantee that an admissions committee will think the worst if left to its own devices."

If you must make an excuse, make it short and sweet. Don't whine. Don't blame anyone else. Just get the facts out and be sure that what you say really holds up. The following essay is a perfect example.

(Name Withheld)
_____

Committee Members:

In order that an accurate scrutinization of my application can be made, I sincerely feel that additional, pertinent information is necessary. I hope this brief description of some of the extremities that have occurred in my background can be of some assistance in your evaluation.

When I was seven years old, my parents were irrevocably divorced. At such an impressionable age, the divorce had a deadening and devastating effect because my father had been my only support system. As the years progressed, I learned of the excruciating, emotional and financial burden it placed on my mother. Being the oldest of four children, there was an ingrown obligation in me to aid my mother in whatever way possible. Four years later in an effort to provide supplemental income to the household, I acquired a paper route. I maintained a paper route during my entire high school career. In addition, I also worked in various part-time capacities at restaurants, car washes and janitorial services. The employment was beneficial to the household, but it totally eliminated my participation in Glee Club, athletics and other high school extra-curricular activities. At the conclusion of my senior year, I was awarded a scholarship from the city newspaper.

For the duration of my collegiate career, my education and the financial stability of my household were contingent on my employment endeavors. My mother had become dependent on me and the monetary contributions I provided became a propriety. More times than not, there was a propensity to let employment and financial circumstances dictate the measure of my individual academic success. One such occasion was the fall semester of 1972. My mother required major surgery and even though insurance covered most of the medical bills, other vital expenses would have been neglected during her recuperation. These circumstances necessitated that I work a full-time job in addition to being a full-time student with work-study employment. Such a stringent schedule proved to be academically detrimental that semester. On several other occasions, it was essential that I maintain full-time employment. Even though the remainder of my career was just as strenuous it was beneficial because it showed the value of time management while serving to foster and cultivate individual perseverance. I received a Bachelor of Arts degree on May 15, 1977.

I was granted admission into a graduate program in 1978. No longer saddled with financial burdens, I was able to excell, complete all requirements and graduate one semester ahead of schedule.

Turning Points:
Essays About Important Changes

How do you use your experiences to change and grow? The "turning point" essay can show how thoughtful, sensitive, and responsive you are, and writing it may give you even more insight.

Unlike Paul on the road to Damascus, one incident rarely changes a person's life. Trying to persuade the reader that a single event suddenly revolutionized your perspective on Life, the Universe, and Everything is likely to sound (and be) contrived rather than profound. Nevertheless, discussing a specific experience can be a great way to express a change or an idea that has developed over time.

The essay by James Silk is especially powerful. His final line—added, it seems, almost casually—jolts the complacent reader. Even if you disagree with him, his essay shows an impressive understanding of issues, emotions, and the perspective on both sides.

Steve Peikin prods the admissions officer with a concluding waiver. Who knows what will happen to Peikin's fragile liberalism without the firm molding of his professors?

Marian Macpherson uses a personal experience to resolve a larger question. With her exposure to Wood's Lab, she realizes that science and art can be compatible rather than antithetical. (Someone should have proofread her essay before she sent it, though.)

Joshua Karsh sprinkles wit throughout his look at another age-old conflict. The twist comes at the end when he surprises the reader expecting yet another religious rebirth.

Finally, Edward Shulman uses a humorous style to describe his search for the meaning of life. The format allows him to explore serious issues without sounding pretentious. If you are going to write about a topic that has been pondered by great minds through the ages, be sure you are thinking in a unique way.

The "turning point" essay demonstrates that you are not obstinate and that you are strong enough to reveal your past ignorance—both admirable traits in a would-be lawyer.

James J. Silk

My students waited for me in our cold, damp classroom. I counted on their unyielding eagerness, wit and warmth and a bit of topicality to dispel the gloom of the Shanghai winter morning. An article in *China Daily* about the execution of a provincial party official for embezzling public money would stimulate a lively discussion. The article drew no response, but my questions about the death penalty elicited a unanimous defense of capital punishment. I clung to undogmatic questioning until my disappointment in the certainty with which even gentle Xiao Chen pronounced judgment outweighed class plans and my commitment to neutrality.

Their arguments never strayed far from the primacy of society over the individual. I recalled American generals observing that life in Asia was simply less dear. My rejection of that cliche undiminished, I was equally unwilling to accommodate the students' views through some more generous exercise of cultural relativism. Despite my appreciation of the cultural, historical and personal sources of their position, I could not leave it unchallenged.

If I referred to the irreversible consequences of a mistake, they assured me that the authorities arrested no one until thorough investigation established certain guilt. My assumption of innocence until proven guilty was not so obvious to them. If I said there was no evidence that capital punishment was an effective deterrent, they said it would deter the kinds of crimes against society that China needed to control. Surely, I said, death is cruel and unusual punishment, grotesquely in excess of the seriousness of such crimes. They found that an arbitrary classification; prison was also cruel and unusual. Furthermore, some crimes so damaged and endangered their fragile, new society that the most extreme punishment was necessary.

I mustered all my eloquence to argue that a state which ratifies death as legal punishment ultimately legitimizes violence and contributes to the very disorder it aims to deter. They responded that not to execute serious offenders was to legitimize the offenses and show the weakness of the state's will.

As class ended, one student dismissed my view as romantically moral, saying, "That's the difference between our cultures. Americans believe there is a right. We believe that what is necessary is right." In frustration at their stale utilitarianism, I resorted to an untestable and petulant last word: "As China develops, your attitude will change." Six months later, I came home to an increasing number of executions in the United States and arguments for them that were merely vengeful.

Steven R. Peikin

"How Can You Defend Those People?"

It is appropriate that James Kunen used this question to title his book about his experiences as an attorney for the Public Defender Service. During my summer as a Yale-P.D.S. Fellow, many people posed the same question to me, and I found myself searching for the answer as well.

I began work at the Public Defender Service feeling uncertain and apprehensive. As an investigator and case assistant for an attorney in the trial division, I was to direct my energies toward the defense of clients charged with serious and violent felony crimes. Our clients might be ex-convicts or drug abusers. On "the other side" stood the U.S. Attorney whose clients were justice, order, and the protection of society. I was not confident that I was on the side of right.

As the summer progressed, however, I witnessed the steady decrease of my uncertainty. My change in attitude reveals some important lessons learned. One of these lessons is that most people, as I did, foster a stereotypical image of "those people." The clients with whom I worked were not all ex-convicts or drug addicts. Nor, as many misconceive, were all of "those people" guilty of the crimes of which they were accused. Certainly many of our clients were guilty, but their guilt in no way precluded their right to the best possible representation. The only commonality which I could observe in our clients was an inability to pay for their own defense.

Anyone working in criminal justice must observe that the system is inherently weighted against poor people. If lawyers are valued by how much money they receive for their services, then poor people are most likely to receive the lowest quality legal representation. The apprehensions that I had about defending "those people" quickly fell before the realization that their poverty causes them to be treated as inferiors before the law. Working to help the small actor assert his or her equality before a large and powerful system seems like a worthwhile service.

My greatest uncertainty about working for P.D.S. stemmed from a preconception that defense attorneys work against the service of justice to let the guilty go unpunished. My conscience was eased by my observation that this is largely untrue. For the most part, the guilty are convicted when the evidence weighs against them. Further, our system of jurisprudence assures that the conviction of the innocent is extremely rare. But does this reality mean that justice prevails? In answering this question, James Kunen makes a very astute, if sobering, observation. He says that by the time a criminal case gets to court, almost all of the injustice has already occurred. "The victim has already been victimized; the defendant, more often than not, has been subjected to every kind of abuse, from inadequate prenatal care to exclusion from the work force." In such a framework, how can any court claim to administer ultimate justice?

During my time at P.D.S. I became extremely sympathetic to our clientele. The murder case that I worked on for most of the summer resulted in an acquittal, and I was extremely proud to have been part of the defense team. Nevertheless, there are aspects of criminal defense which still trouble me. Removed from the environment of P.D.S., many of my doubts about the role of defense attorney return. I anticipate that my legal education will enable me to explore this problem further and will allow me to consider it in a more enlightened perspective.

Marian Macpherson

What I Learned in Wood's Lab

At the Universtiy of the South there is a mysterious place called Wood's Lab where English majors do not go. Being a loyal and enthusiastic English major, myself, I conscientiously shunned Wood's Lab until, one day, when, near the end of my fifth semester, I placed myself into a situation which would not only recquire me to enter that ominous building, but which would also teach me a valuable lesson about the relationship between the study of the arts, to which I was devoted, and the study of the sciences, from which I was trying to disassociate myself.

My adventure began when, while looking through the course list for my next semester's classes, I came upon the intriguing title "Cultural Anthropology of Appalachia and the South". Having grown up in the South, I am always interested in learning more about it, and this course, which proposed specifically to examine our culture, demanded my serious consideration. Although I saw that this course was scheduled to meet in Wood's Lab, I read the course description. When I discovered that William Faulkner's *The Sound and the Fury* was listed among the recquired texts, temptation and curiosity overcame my inhibitions. I registered to take Anthropology 309.

As the day of my first meeting approached, I began with horror to consider the ramifications of what I had done. I was going to have to orient myself to a whole new mode of thinking. Grammatical rules would not help me now. I was going to be on my own, surrounded by "scientific" people, in the dreaded Wood's Lab. It was a great relief when I finally attended the first class and realized that all my fears had been groundless. The interior of Wood's Lab was as comfortable and as aesthetically pleasing as those of the buildings in which I took my English and French classes. The "scientific" people expressed themselves in comprehendible, even eloquent, terms, and the subject matter was just as interesting as I had hoped it would be. I learned much about the culture of which I am a part, but more importantly I learned that my literary background could complement my anthropological studies, just as my experience in Wood's Lab could enhance my appreciation of literature and the arts. My anthropology class exposed me to a whole new realm of insights into *The Sound and the Fury*, and in writing my final paper on the development of Southern Literaure as a distinct art form I found that there is an unbreakable bond between the study of art and that of science. The two are inextricably linked in a complex network of overlaps and divergences. To look at only one aspect of the network is to prevent yourself from seeing the whole truth of what you are studying. For anyone to say honestly that he has a liberal arts education, he must be able to view the world from a liberal perspective. By venturing into Wood's Lab, I gained this perspective, and I will graduate from Sewanee in May, with the solid background I need to begin pursuit of a law degree.

Joshua Karsh

Towards the end of spring semester last year, posters appeared around campus announcing an "Ivy League Torah Study Program." The Lubavitcher Chasidim were offering select, Jewish college students an eight-week crash course in faith, *Chasidus*, and the world of our great-grandparents. My reading of Kierkegaard should no doubt have dissuaded me from such a program, but the chance to scout the faith-fed mind from the inside caught my fancy, and I signed on. Pitting three years of Ivy liberal arts education against eight weeks of Chasidic *yiddishe yeshiva* indoctrination, I reasoned that if the yeshiva were to win, my parents might at least file for malpractice against Yale in retaliation.

On the day of my campus interview, still elated by the tropes tossed out by my literature professor an hour before, I hurried into Career Services and headed toward the waiting area, where a lone, rabbinic-looking figure, barely visible behind his shaggy beard and underneath his black hat, stood mumbling Psalms to himself in a corner. "Text" was about to confront "Torah"; Yale to meet yeshiva. The Chasid in the corner looked up, and we greeted each other. That, however, was the last I said for several minutes, as he zealously prepared to set me straight. All the while waving his body back and forth, my Chasid began to explain that in spite of the "critical heresies" I had just heard propounded in the classroom, where the Torah was concerned the Author would always defy the deconstruction of a Derrida. I listened patiently, nodded, suggested to this Chasid that the two of us had been nurtured on the same tastes of shmaltz and the same bedtime stories, and then offered that while I personally doubted whether the formula could be found which would square my view of things with his, I was still eager to see our shared palates and imaginations give it a try. He leaned back, whispered, "Have a little faith," and smiled.

Ten weeks later, I and sixteen other college *buchers* sat down opposite five rabbis, most of us to *"lerne"* the ways of their religious minds, most of them to rescue us from lapsed thought and act. Not surprisingly, certain snags soon appeared: "What about the archaeological evidence of this 7000-year-old ...?" *"Nu, vat by it?"* "Well, you claim the world is just 5700 years old ..." *"Nu, nu?"* .... The difficulty was plain: for these spiritual virtuosos, the only logic linking one proposition to the next was faith; but for me, the *logic* of faith was inscrutable. Borrowings from Tertullian's creed—*Credo, quia absurdum est* (these rabbis could only believe it *because* it was so absurd)—kept rushing through my mind, as I struggled to appreciate what it must be like to operate according to rabbinic logic, to find one's psyche tortured by crucifixion envy and one's intellect covenanted to a circumcision of reason. I did not think that I would ever understand.

The marvel, however, was that before long I did begin to understand. I even began to wish that I too might float—like the rabbis—on logical lacunae, might walk—like the rabbis—on water, so to speak. In the face of rabbinic virtuosity, all my old rules, all my old skepticisms, seemed to give way. Though theretofore "religiously unmusical" (Max Weber), I found myself suddenly yearning to chant and sing anyway, abruptly and unexpectedly persuaded that the songs the rabbis were teaching would somehow make harmonies of my confused and insistent dichotomies. Clashes such as those between fact and value, deed and creed, content and intent, art and act, and signifier and signified, all looked as if they might finally achieve resolution; for the rabbis' songs, like no others I had ever heard or learned, seemed to promise special secrets of sense, and of meaning. Daily, absurdity was becoming more manageable.

For weeks, then, I fought in earnest to learn to sing with the rabbis, to chant their tunes. But, foolishly, I mistook the proper tack. To sing, I figured, one surely had to sit down and practice the notes. So I sat down, and I practiced. But the notes finished, unavoidably, by blocking rather than clearing my way. Indeed, it was a long while until I realized what Kierkegaard should have made clear for me before, that one does not **learn**, or even *lerne*, to chant the tunes of the rabbis. Those tunes are **willed**; and he who would truly chant them must do so from the deeps of the soul, where no notes are ever found.

In the end, in the classrooms where I spend my time today, I am still learning from notes of sorts, and I am still battling the same dichotomies. But after my summer with the rabbis, I know now that neither notes nor dichotomies, nor the bulk of a college education, lend anything to the search for faith. Man may find many things by knowledge; but he finds faith only by unconditionally willing it. Unfortunately, willing like that amounts to volitional suicide; and I am not up to it. But oh, I wish that I were.

Edward G. Shulman

... A long time ago, in an age that has been all but forgotten, there was an ordinary man who was on a quest. This was a quest unlike any other seen before. It was not for gold, nor was it for women. It was for a prize that only a few heroic men ever dared to challenge. The quest was for the truth, and the man's name if you haven't guessed already was Sir Edward of Livinshire.

Edward was like most young men in Livinshire. He would go to the Jousting events at the local park, and every now and then, he could be seen shooting arrows at a target, behind the schoolyard. This was not enough for Edward. He needed more. He needed to learn. Young Edward left the small village of Livinshire to seek knowledge in a distant land known as Syrayork.

Syrayork overwhelmed the young man. He found that his time was monopolized by many activites, such as attending wild parties thrown by the Greeks. Edward understood too late that the activites in which he participated hindered his learning. Edward, little by little, became accustomed to his surroundings. He read the works of the great scholars and learned to master the written word. Edward realized that he had come to Syrayork as an immature boy, and he was leaving as a knowledgeable man. There was still something missing. Edward was not satisfied with what he had acquired. He needed more.

Edward decided to return home. On his way, he realized that he was always the student and never the teacher. Edward decided to teach. This was the missing piece to the puzzle. Teaching would be a new beginning. He could take innocent minds, and mold them into something special. This satisfied Edward for a period of time, but it was not a constant challenge for him. He needed something, that would continually test his mind. Teaching was not the answer. Sir Edward was in a quandry. He was young, yet he was still searching. Searching for the truth. He was on a quest.

Edward travelled to many different lands, and he examined many different cultures. He saw the peasants of Russia, as well as, the natives of the Hawaiian Islands. He witnessed the hardships of people less fortunate than himself. He saw that freedom is a valuable gift that is often taken for granted. Traveling gave Edward new insight into other peoples problems. However, he could not solve his own dilemma.

Edward started to feel that there was no such thing as the truth. But, he still continued in his pursuit for that valuable prize. The answer finally hit him, while he was sitting under an apple tree. The solution was in front of him the whole time. The law is the truth. The law which is often ridiculed, still keeps order in the world. If there is no law, there would be no justice. If there is no justice, then we would not be humans anymore. We would be animals. The law is what keeps men civilized.

With these things in mind, Edward began a new quest. A quest to find a land in which he could study the law. This ends Part I of the story, Part II will be written in the near future.

So You Want To Be a Lawyer:
Essays About Entering the Legal Profession

Why should the resources of a great law school be devoted to you? Why should you get the thick packet next March while 10,000 other applicants get only a thin letter?

One way to convince admissions officers that you do deserve a space at their school is to discuss why you want to be there in the first place. People choose to become lawyers for many reasons. If your reason is interesting and revealing of your character, it might make a great essay.

The first four of these essays concern idealistic visions. The writers claim that a law degree might empower them to give life to their dreams of better justice, clean sports, social morality, or better education.

But weary admissions officers can get cynical about proclamations of social conscience (after all, does anyone support worse justice or unfair sports?), so be sure to support your assertions with concrete actions or anecdotes. Note that in R. Scott Taylor's piece, the story of his grandfather's carpentry business actually gives the applicant credibility. Sensitivity to the actions of others can be more powerful than a list of your own great deeds.

The writers of the next essays are driven by their own restlessness—the search for meaning or stimulation. Such a motivation can be compelling, but take care not to grow too ponderous. Few admissions directors want to give a scarce opening to someone who is exploring without purpose and direction. "If an applicant wants to search himself," one told us, "he should take a year off and travel or something. Law school is demanding, and if students are confused about why they're there, problems will arise. Only occasionally will intellectual curiosity itself be enough to warrant admission."

Whether you agree with that policy or not, you must be sensitive to a school's perspective. Never just say you are "just looking." State your purpose in positive terms: "I want a broad legal training that will allow me to enter many new fields." If you're not sure why you're going to law school, avoid the subject. Better yet, perhaps, reconsider your entire application.

R. Scott Taylor

The Taylor's have been carpenters on the island of Nantucket since the days of Ahab. I broke the tradition; I proved inept. They sent me "to America", to prep school. I came to Wesleyan thinking that I'd major in economics, go into business. I bid on the lease for a beachhouse and turned it into a small restaurant. The venture was a financial success but it slaked my entrepreneurial spirit. As a sophomore my consciousness was raised while discovering feminism, socialism, and learning group process. My major became English. The following year was spent on academic lease, studying Scandinavian literature and social welfare at the University of Stockholm. I returned committed to working for social change. The last two years I have worked with NRG, the Wesleyan Men's Community, and SAFE, the Middlesex County Rape Crisis Center (I'm a male counselor). I most enjoy the interpersonal relationships and counselling of being a freshperson adviser.

I don't aspire to fame or fortune. I want to work with people, for people, to be a public advocate, to practice law with the emphasis on counselor. As an introduction to a life of poverty and frustration I am currently working as an intern to the Appropriations Committee of the financially strapped 1981 session of the Connecticut General Assembly. To keep my idealism alive I'll be facilitating (officially a Teaching Apprentice) a student-run course at Wesleyan called "Towards a Socialist America", while remaining a freshperson adviser.

In 1934 Elmore Taylor took over his father's carpentry business with thirty dollars and a set of tools. He wanted to build the best carpentry firm on the island. In 1980 when he passed that business on to my father it employed nine men. He had never used a bookkeeper, nor a typewriter, nor even a pen. It was not the biggest carpentry firm on the island, nor the busiest, but it was, he assured me, the best. I want to practice law as my grandfather practiced his trade. He never billed anyone twice. If they didn't pay the first time he assumed that there were extenuating circumstances and forgot about it. Repairs for charitable organizations were always done gratis. Compensating with analytic dexterity for what I lack in manual dexterity, I am genuinely excited about studying law and anxious to put that knowledge to work in a socially responsible way. Northeastern has created one of the few law school environments from which I could emerge with my social morality intact, maybe even enhanced. It is one of the few law schools with a conscience. I would like to be a part of that environment. Elmore would be proud.

Thomas William Andrews

As I have grown older, the Constitution of the United States of America has become, for me, a sort of secular religious document. At the risk of sounding ridiculous, some people dream of joining the clergy, I dream of joining the bar. Some people feel drawn to Mecca or the Wailing Wall, I was drawn to visit Washington, D.C. and the glass-encased Constitution.

The Constitution is one of the things in this world that I choose to use to give definition to my life. I once tried to memorize it, but now I simply strive to understand it. I bought a facsimile of the Constitution in the gift shop of the building where George Washington was sworn in as our first President. It hangs on my wall as in other homes one might find a crucifix or Menorah on the mantel.

I have heard people criticize the number of lawyers in the United States. The standard, simplistic comparison used is the ratio of lawyers to engineers in both America and Japan. While it is true that the United States has far more lawyers than any other society on the planet Earth, it seems also evident that we enjoy more justice than any other society on this planet.

We need people who know the law, and who push for justice, and who are uncompromising toward our freedom and rights. I feel there is always room for one more good lawyer. I want to be one of the people in our society trying to make the Constitution work, exercising our rights, and keeping freedom a strong and viable force.

Michael Harrington

"Al McGuire's Halftime Hoops" begins as the camera picks up the NBC-Sports commentator walking across the beautiful North Carolina campus with alumni and Sports Attorney Michael K. Harrington.

McGuire: Walking around here Mike, does it bring back memories?

Harrington: Yes Al, and every memory is a positive one.

McGuire: What made you choose to be a Sports Lawyer?

Harrington: Many things Al. I always participated in athletics myself and truly love the game of basketball. I guess I never really wanted to lose touch with sports. I also realized that there existed grave problems within the Sports Management arena. So I thought to myself that something had to be done to correct the wrongdoings of agents, and envisioned that I would be the man to achieve such a claim. Therefore, in many ways I rooted for the perpetuation of such corruption, solely because I wanted to provide the cure.

McGuire: You once said that your undergraduate schooling was chiefly responsible for your decision. How is that?

Harrington: Two reasons. First, I think that Williams College . . .

McGuire: The only school to ever deny John Wooden as a Coach.

Harrington: The same. Incredible, right? Anyway, Williams allowed me to discover who I was. The smallness of the school breeds self-understanding, while also facilitating association with many others. Essentially, I learned a great deal about human beings and this enabled me to empathize with the plight of young athletes. I figured that if I was under pressure at 20, then so were they. Second, you have to remember that I was at Williams when Sports Agent controversies truly came out into the open. During my Junior year alone, both Chris Carter and Derrick Mckey, All-Americans in football and basketball respectively, lost their final year of eligibility because they signed contracts too early.

McGuire: Did you find that North Carolina, specifically, helped you prepare for your future?

Harrington: Aside from my own knowledge and love of sports, North Carolina has meant everything. The legal training and education that I received from NC was outstanding, for it prepared me fully for my encounters in the "real world." Additionally, and very importantly, was the contact and exposure to the sports program at North Carolina, truly one of the most disciplined and demanding in the country. In fact, I benefitted immensely from my association with Coach Smith, who allowed me inside the basketball program where I could further discover the mindset of the young athlete.

McGuire: You are currently doing very well. Are you satisfied?

Harrington: Yes, I am. You know, Al, the tendency in America is to measure success by how much money you make. To me, success means that I have helped a young and gifted, but vulnerable, athlete on the right path to a promising future. Realistically, Sports Law is a business for me, and I have to behave like a businessman sometimes. Fortunately, not that often. Thus far I have done very well without forgetting my purpose. It is very satisfying and comforting to know that I can be "successful" in this business without breaking the NCAA or Professional rules. I am very proud of this, and elated to see more and more athletes adhering to the rules.

McGuire: Have you realized your Dream?

Harrington: One of them, yes, I would like to think. If I have made athletes more aware of the consequences of signing early or accepting money, and been responsible for any one athlete to follow the rules, then I think my dream is realized.

McGuire: What's your other dream?

Harrington: To take your job away from you! (Laughter)

McGuire: Thanks alot for your time and good luck in your future.

Harrington: Thank you Al. GO HEELS!!

(Name Withheld)

Currently, I hold a bachelor's degree in history and philosophy, and a master's degree in American Studies, from Purdue University, and I am a doctoral candidate in Educational Foundations, Policy and Administration at the University of Michigan. My primary interest in law arose from my studies of the organization and operation of American schools. Legal questions lie at the heart of nearly all controversies in public and private education; legal remedies, therefore, play a significant role in the resolution of these controversies. Also, many different forms of legal controversies are involved in education; there are contractural issues, other labor-management issues, and constitutional issues raised there on a regular basis. I wish to pursue a law degree for the practical purpose of helping to resolve these disputes and hopefully to contribute to the ongoing improvement of American education and education in Indiana in particular.

Since 1983 and the publication of several national reports critical of American education, state and local leaders have been re-examining their own educational programs and many have been making changes for the better. Laws governing education at the state level are a central element in maintaining a healthy system. And people who know the law and are committed to the area and to the health of the system are just as important. Having lived in central Indiana for eleven of the last thirteen years I have become settled here, have become committed to its development, and have come to know this area very well. In October of 1987 I was elected to the Board of Directors by the membership of the West Side Food Cooperative and as the Board secretary by the members of the Board. From this position I have been able to begin to gain a greater understanding not only of business management but of the surrounding community, as well.

My teaching, research, and writing experience have all helped prepare me for legal training. For two years as a graduate student at Purdue University I worked as a teaching assistant in the two-course sequence in American Constitutional History. I have also taught introduction to American History, at Purdue University, and Education in a Multi-Cultural Society at the University of Michigan, each of which necessarily dealt with legal affairs. I have gained considerable experience in legal research from graduate school coursework, as well as from research outside specific courses. This year, for instance, I assisted in the production of a Danforth Foundation conference paper on challenges to U.S. Supreme Court rulings on educational issues.

(Name Withheld)

Like many, I suspect, who have been born into opportunity—into relative affluence and some intelligence—I have
had difficulty eliminating the possible. This may not be a wor-
thy lament, but it is a genuine one, one which has claimed
much of the eighteen or so months following my graduation
from college.

The typical college student comes upon graduation as upon a
precipice, and many months of obsessive communal anticipa-
tion somehow fail to mitigate the abruptness of that moment
in which he or she finally toes its edge. For the Summa cum
Laude graduate of an elite school, this precipice is high indeed:
so high, in fact, that he is told "the world is at his feet." At his
back, thrusting him forward, is a life of high achievemnent on a
carefully mapped, gently sloped course. Before him is, well,
everything. A keen sense of incipient adventure might con-
stitute an admirable response to such a predicament. Dizziness
would not be inappropriate.

My own sense of vertigo upon leaving Dartmouth was
steepened by conflicting forces within my personality. These
cross-currents appear to me now as quite distinct, and their
respective origins are easy to trace. From my mother I have inherited an impulse which one might generously deem 'artistic'.
It prescribes a disengaged but highly sensitized observation of
the world, a perception that is oblique and highly personal. It
involves but it does not implicate. There is a certain unclut-
tered freshness to its vision.

From my father I have inherited a grasping analytical
curiosity as to the 'how' of things, an urge to explore and
penetrate the workings, the machinations, of government and
business and other sectors of our society. This current demands
that one get in there and mix it up. It aspires to competence in
the ways of the world, delighting, exulting even, in an involve-

ment that is both intimate and intricate. It is the force which energizes the 'problem solver'.

These two impulses subscribe to different kinds of vision and strive for different kinds of understanding. If integrated, intuition tells me, they carry the promise of a rare and powerful synergy. Left in turmoil, I am equally sure, they can confuse, dispirit, and ultimately even paralyze.

You can probably envision me as I left school, bubbling like a cauldron. I was unwilling to emulate the precise and, as I saw it, mainly uninformed steps of my classmates. My ideas were broader. I had invested my high school earnings in the stock market at the beginning of this latest protracted bull market and so felt that, for a while at least, I could afford broad ideas. I thought in terms of 'exposure', which, it turns outs, I was to acquire through a series of false starts. A year's exposure to a foreign culture and language was cut off at six weeks thanks to newly stringent French labor laws and a companion's change of plans. Next I sought exposure to journalism and to New York City. I was exposed to (in?) New York for only three months, as my exploration of journalism there was limited to a basketfull of 'not hiring' notices (not to mention a daily scouring of *The New York Times*). At this point I was ready to come in from the cold for a time, which meant returning home and resuming my work as an editorial and research assistant on a projected Law School textbook, just then consigned to a new round of revision. My efforts here focused on the metaphysical labyrynth of intellectual property law as applied to computer software and hardware. It was familiar and engaging work and lasted until the project was terminated.

Ultimately, 'exposure' came to mean exposure to myself. The vehicle for this final definition was my decision to indulge a lifelong fantasy by devoting a year to writing fiction. Writing fiction consists largely of eliminating the possible, which makes it good practice for post-graduate living. The rest of such writing is, paradoxically, the preservation of the possible. As you might guess, I am most adept at this second task. I have been engaged in balancing those two objectives for several months under the cover of an eclectic range of occupations (ice cream man, waiter etc.). I am not quite sure what to make of the product of these efforts (an ambivalence which, I assure you, does not extend to waiting tables). But I have no doubt the experiment has been worthwhile. It's value inheres not so much in the daily exercise of writing itself, or even in the product of that exercise, but rather in the decision to step into the world calling oneself, sincerely, a 'writer'. The fallout from this commitment constitutes something like a visit to certain new age beauty parlors. One emerges, I imagine, with the wax removed from one's ears, the hair snipped away from one's eyes, and an entirely new layer of skin to meet the breeze.

In the end, however, more than anything else, writing means returning to oneself. It is thus among the loneliest and most self-indugent of occupations. And, at this point in life, there is a discomfitting pretentiousness to it, as well. One can wallow in one's own existence for only so long, and I'm beginning to recognize a need to get out of that mud.

Sometimes the dizziness of the recent graduate gives way slowly to the vaguest kind of disappointment, an amorphous burden attached somehow to the irrevocable linear momentum of living. He or she comes to realize, perhaps with undue emphasis, that each step taken is done so to the exclusion of all others. To walk through one doorway is to imagine hearing a thousand other doors slam shut. The only way to preserve pure possibility, that state of mind in which the talented and open minded undergrad peruses his own potential, is to stand perfectly still, which, of course, gets you precisely nowhere. For one born at the alter of opportunity, this discovery that freedom does not feel like freedom can be as unsettling as betrayal.

I wish I could say I am applying to Law School as part of some grand scheme to change the world, to leave it a little more just or even a little more efficient. But I am not sure such a thing is feasible, at least by design. Nothing is quite so neat for me. This is instead very much a personal decision, one inspired by my own needs, certain and uncertain. I have thought long and hard about how best to reconcile my disparate natures. And I am doing my best to eliminate the possible in favor of the actual.

Charles E. Valles

Socrates once said, "An unexamined life is not worth living." Well, here it goes.

For the first eighteen years of my life, my parents led the tedious task of convincing their only child that an uneducated individual was mercilessly destined to lead an unsuccessful life. In the Valles household, Education = Money = Success = Happiness. The beneficial qualities of an enlightened mind were secondary considerations, instead, primitive scare tactics were employed. How vividly the memories of youth endure...

... standing at my mother's side in line at the neighborhood Taco Bueno, and to suddenly hear that soft, protective, maternal voice approach my eager, impressionable young ears and whisper something like, "Charles, do you see that cook behind the counter, the one with the tatoo and the earring and no teeth?" Oh, so slowly I would raise up on my toes and peer, neck outstretched, until I managed to locate the unfortunate subject of the day's session of 'LESSON IN LIFE, PART 783', and having done so, would turn back to my mother and, anticipating yet another horrifying story, would hesitantly respond "Yes, mommy?" Now my mother, never one to be accused of sanding down rough edges would say, "I'll bet you a dollar," one of her favorite expressions, "that he never finished school, has at least ten or twenty illegitimate children, is an habitual dope addict, doesn't have the slightest clue where his mother is, is probably wanted by every law enforcement agency in the western hemisphere," and for the grand finale, "and will be working at this SAME JOB FOR THE SAME PAY twenty years from now, that is if he doesn't murder everyone in the place one afternoon." Quizzically, I would again peer up and over the counter for another glance, quietly praying to the heavens that this would not be the fateful afternoon which would witness such misery, at least until my mother and I were safely distanced from this psychopathic haven.

For the first eighteen years of my life, I enjoyed the material benefits of a thriving Texas oil economy. Particularly throughout my high school years, a generous parental pocketbook, with the exception of working a few hours a week at my father's real estate office, replaced the vile necessity of sacking groceries at the neighborhood Safeway. However, growing up economically OVER-advantaged had serious unanticipated drawbacks. When I graduated from high school, I had simply had no desire to continue. I was bored with academics. My world became centered around athletic excellence and soccer expertise, and it was to this end that I dedicated my ambitions. From the time I was eleven years old I had planned to get my real estate license after high school and begin working for my father, an idea which my parents had gradually come to accept. Only when the world oil glut sent the Texas economy spinning did a college degree become a realistic probability. Not until one month before the first day of classes in the fall of 1984 was I absolutely sure that I would be attending college. An advanced education had become a sudden, cruel necessity, not a welcomed endeavor.

It was no surprise, then, when I decided to enter S.M.U. What better place to spend four years than at a university since referred to by the *New York Times* as 'Camp Wonderland', where the lobby of the new student union features marble tables and Persian rugs, and a shuttle service is operated, despite the size of the campus, to insure that our Reebok's don't wear out too quickly. I was prepared for a four year vacation and I got stung, period.

For the lack of nothing better to do, I began to pursue a degree in business. Quite honestly, it was the most miserable experience of my life, an experience which was accurately reflected by my performance in the first three semesters. What material I did absorb was committed to short term memory for test purposes, and soon thereafter forgotten. In the Spring semester of my sophomore year, quite by luck, I registered in an American Government and Politics course. It was my saving grace. After three semesters of memorizing methods of calculating depreciaton and interest rates, I was exposed to the opportunity of expanding intellectually, to analyze and criticize, not merely memorize. Faced with an opportunity for what I saw to be a refreshing change of pace, I began to wholeheartedly to exploit the liberal education, and redirected my degree plan toward Political Science. Slowly, I was able to focus the ambitions and desires which had carried me across the soccer field for so many years into a desire to broaden my mind. The resulting change in academic performance was tremendous.

My last four semesters of studies have shown that I have an intellectual potential which has only begun to emerge. The liberal arts degree has fostered the growth of critical skills of evaluation as instruments of reasoning. Combined with a healthy exposure to both business and economics, and an active participation in extracurricular and cocurricular activities, the liberal arts curriculum has provided a course and means of self discovery. Paradoxically, more education has left me less satisfied than did my high school experience. Learning has become an obsession. As a student at the Boston University School of Law, I will continue to pursue my current journey toward intellectual expansion and excellence.

(Name Withheld)

When I graduated from college four years ago, I found myself someplace I wasn't really prepared to be—the real world. Suddenly bills had to be paid, and a job had to replace the ritual of going to classes. I went out bravely in search of the perfect job—one that would pay the bills *and* stimulate every fiber of my being.

That first summer after college I worked as a receptionist in the mornings and a retail sales person at night. I paid my bills, but I had a hard time imagining myself doing the work I was doing for the rest of my life. I moved on to other jobs: for a while I was a child care specialist and a cocktail waitress, then I became a secretary and a paperboy (woman). I had excellent credit rating, but no sense of fulfillment.

This summer I took a temporary job in a law office in Northampton, Massachusetts. I had just finished a stint as a governess in the Boston area and needed a job while I reevaluated my goals and pondered the meaning of life.

For three weeks I went to work at the law office and, for the first time, was genuinely stimulated by the work. My boss, a traffic lawyer, encouraged me to return on a full-time basis after a planned trip to the Midwest, and I did. I was made his legal aide, and have been involved with cases and clients and the why's and how's of law ever since. I look forward to going to work each day because I'm challenged. This challenge and what lies at the heart of it—helping people—is why I'd like to study law.

(Name Withheld)

My reason for wanting to study law are manifold, yet they all focus on the same end—a fuller realization of my utility as a person, mother, wife, worker and citizen. Since first encountering it many years ago, I am still struck by the wisdom in a aphorism of Benjamin Franklin, which I will paraphrase here— "the measure of a thing's worth is its utility."

As a person, I have been given, and have attempted to continue developing, a certain intelligence. I feel that it is my personal responsibility to extend this development and to now focus it on the study of law. After working for nearly five years in this field, I am more intrigued than ever with the law—what are its bases? its rules? its theory? its application? Working within the field has whetted my appetite to learn the hows and whys of law. I am increasingly frustrated with my daily work, which is tangential to the practice of the law; I am much more interested in reading and analyzing the arguments in a pleading than getting it neatly filed away. On a purely personal level, I will be a more satisfied and challenged person—a more *useful* one—if, after my formal study of the law, I can join what I learn with my life experience and intelligence to yield a more highly productive individual.

As a mother, I have provided the customary support, love and guidance to my children. I began and finished my undergraduate work during the years that my sons were quite young, and I believe that we have all benefited from the process. Although my parents are not college graduates, my sons regard a college education as a given. In our home, we customarily talk about ideas. The children have been nurtured on questioning, analyzing, critiquing and proposing alternative solutions. My study of law will not be isolated; the children will be included and they will grow in insight and aspiration as a result.

Having a husband who is an attorney has proved to be an invaluable source of information. Many of our conversations center around legal issues. I know that my study of the law will augment, refresh and clarify my husband's understanding of the subject, while his growing practical knowledge will certainly supplement my effectiveness. My law school experience will be a truly family affair.

As a member of society, a worker and a citizen, I feel that practicing as an attorney will more nearly fulfill my potential to contribute to my generation, my country and the future. I am sure that the study of law will sharpen and deepen my understanding and respect for the principles upon which our society is founded.

To sum up, I feel that my study of law has a unity of purpose. It will yield not only personal growth and self-realization, but will enhance the intellectual and social development of my sons, provide my husband a sounding board (and sometimes, a foil), and produce in us at least five more useful members of society, better citizens all. In years to come, I intend that this benefit have a wider application through service to the profession and the larger community.

(Name Withheld)

The picture of Neil Armstrong first walking on the moon is
still ingrained on my mind. It was seeing him on the moon
that created my desire to leave the ground. As a child, I used
to watch airplanes fly overhead, all the while dreaming that
someday I too could leave the shackles of the ground. After
years of dreaming, I can fly. I can leave the ground and fly into
the blue infinity. The serenity of flying above the beautiful
earth, above the rush of people, is quite relaxing. I knew as a
child that I would love flying; I just did not know how much.

I dreamed other dreams as a child. I dreamed of becoming a
policeman, a fireman, an astronaut, and an attorney. All but
the latter dream have fallen from view. My interest in law and
the legal profession has only increased since childhood. In college, I found my interests and abilities to be closely matched in
law related areas. I need to know that the work I am doing
makes a difference. After spending two years in the business
school, I found the emphasis on the bottom line to be less than
fulfilling.

I also enjoy challenging myself. I like going beyond what I
am currently capable of doing. One of my greatest challenges is
helping people. In my fraternity, I have been fortunate enough
to hold leadership positions from Parliamentarian to President.
I find no greater joy than helping others achieve their goals. I
use all of my abilities to their fullest when leading others. Being involved in extracurricular activites has improved my interpersonal and public speaking skills. It has also helped me to
look more closely at all sides of an issue, to be more objective. I
have learned through my leadership positions how to make difficult decisions. I have gained experience through extra-
curricular activities that hours in the library could never have
taught. The challenge and experience gained from these activities has only encouraged me to continue my involvement in

law school.

The summer jobs I have held have not only put money in my pocket, but they have also helped affirm my desire to attend law school. For three summers, I worked for an electronics supply company. The work involved numbers and limited human contact. It was not challenging. For one summer, I worked as an intern for a state games competition. The hours were long and the work difficult. It was all worth it, though, to see the happy faces of both children and adults at the opening ceremony and during the Olympic style games. Working with people is much more challenging.

From flying to triathloning to practicing law, I need to know I am doing things I enjoy, that I am doing things that are challenging. I am ready to start a new education, one to which I have long been looking forward. I may not be able to walk on the moon, but I am able to contribute in my own way, by becoming an attorney.

In Honor Of Mario Cuomo: Contemplative Essays

The serious, philosophical "thought essay" is perhaps the most difficult to write. The best examples demonstrate an intellectually curious and disciplined mind, but even the best can be hard to read. Frequently, the work loses its impact because students digress from the original point and allow their logic to become muddled by "$10 words" and complicated strings of sentences.

Most students get too abstract when they discuss philosophical concepts. When you write about abstract ideas, link the idea to a tangible example with which the reader can identify. For example, you might use the death of a friend as a starting point for a discussion of religious philosophy. Remember, too, that admissions officers are pressed for time. They don't have all day to kick back and mull over your deep, brilliant insights.

Emily Nozick, for instance, sticks to eating habits and animals—things familiar to everyone—to illustrate how she has developed her philosophy and reconciled emotion with intellect.

Notice that she begins with a line calculated to perplex the reader without confusing him. After reading her first sentence, you're not sure what she's talking about, but you want to keep reading. She piques your interest, and reading her essay becomes a pleasure, not a chore.

What if Nozick had written a more typical, "safe" essay on the same topic? Her first line might read something like this: "Throughout the history of mankind, the intellect and the emotion, two characteristics which uniquely define the human in the animal world, have been locked in conflict . . . "

Want to read more?

Interestingly, when we asked students to submit essays to us, a high number were "thought essays," and almost all were tough to read. But when admissions officers sent us their favorite essays, only a few were philosophical. After all, if you were forced to read 300 essays a day, would you rather read Immanuel Kant or Mark Twain?

We don't want to scare you, though. The "thought essay" can be both interesting and effective. But write clearly and make sure that your ideas follow in a fluid manner. Don't make assumptions about the reader's knowledge, and be careful not to make mental leaps which leave the reader with brain cramps.

At the same time, you cannot risk sounding pedantic or unsophisticated. Lecturing on the law—before you have studied it—is likely to bore and irritate the reader. No matter how great your contributions will be someday, it is far safer—and more revealing—to discuss your vision than your knowledge.

Emily Nozick

The material of my shoes has always been a point of discomfort for me, and the subject has arisen a remarkable number of times in conversation. It is not that my shoes are made of anything unusual, they are made of leather, but when I claim to be a vegetarian on moral grounds, one of the first attacks is always aimed at my feet.

I am never quite sure how to respond to this accusation of hypocrisy and I have fallen back on the idea that I am "doing what I can", although I do not hold my head high when I give this retort. At the same time, however, I am somewhat taken aback by their response. It seems that, although I have never voiced it as anything other than a personal choice, people are automatically defensive around vegetarians, and seek either to explain their own eating habits ("I only eat red meat twice a week") or to attack mine ("I've heard that plants scream when you cut them"). Why does vegetarianism elicit such a probing series of questions about exactly what you eat, what your grounds are, and how you justify other areas of your life? Does punching a hole in my behavior enable others to eat their hamburger in peace? Inconsistency in practice, it seems, is the downfall of any theory.

Nonetheless, the questioning has forced me to examine my views, and to reevaluate my original reasons for holding them. I first made up my mind to stop eating meat, chicken, and fish at our Thanksgiving table when I was three. No elaborately reasoned theory contributed to this decision; no pro-con arguments were weighed in my mind. I reacted from pure emotion. I had just seen a live turkey, who was looking perfectly content with his life, and here was an almost unrecognizable turkey, inert on the table. It just did not seem fair. But while my "this turkey wanted to live" statement adequately captured the line of reasoning of a three year old, I no longer feel comfortable maintaining a toddler's view of the world. At 20 years old, I feel pressured, both from others and from myself, to present a perfectly coherent picture of my sympathy for animals. Either the belief must encompass my practices of wearing leather and killing cockroaches in the bathroom, or my practices must change.

Unfortunately, a flawless system of action is not easy to obtain. Either the theory has gaping holes, or the practice is just too strenuous and demanding. But isn't remaining faithful to a spotted theory intellectually dishonest? How can inconsistency in action be explained?

With vegetarianism, I have to admit that in addition to the issue of inconvenience, my actions reveal the triumph of emotions over intellect. I do what I *feel* driven to do, and I ignore what I am ambivalent towards. I feel a "turn of the stomach" at the thought of eating meat, and not at the idea, or the action, of wearing leather. I certainly do not feel repulsion at killing a cockroach, in fact, I am disgusted by the idea of letting it roam free. All of my life I have acted on this one feeling of not wanting to eat animals and I have not worried about the actions surrounding it. Perhaps it is artificial to now start molding some all-encompassing theory out of pure emotion. For even if I succeed in creating a view to fit my practices or vice-versa, feelings of apathy or disgust have the first and final vote in this issue for me.

This is interesting, because in so many aspects of my life I hold up reason as supreme. I myself, like those who criticize me, have always had contempt for hypocrisy, or even an appeal to psychology over intellect. Such practices seemed weak. And here I am falling into the trap of irrationality of the very issue which, on the surface, stands on a pure intellectual decision. But to be honest, although it may be weak, I really think that emotion ultimately motivates my choice. After 17 years of being a vegetarian, and of thinking that it is "right", for whatever reasons, it is a part of me. I am comfortable with this belief and no amount of prodding can shake me from the emotion. I guess that while intellect grows between the ages of 3 and 20, emotions stay pretty much the same.

Elia Fischer

In his essay "Can Retributivists Support Legal Punishment," in the April 1980 issue of *Monist*, George Schedler argues that a retributivist cannot consistently condemn telishment as unjust while supporting a system of legal punishment. Telishment, which is the inflicting of punishment on innocent people for an ulterior motive, has been objected to by retributivists in that doing so is inherently unjust. Schedler argues that since all systems of legal punishment will, on occasion, mistakenly punish innocent people, consistency demands of the retributivist that he reject all systems of legal punishment and not only telishment.

Schedler's argument contains two minor fallacies which I will discuss before elaborating upon the major flaw in his argument. His assumption that all systems of legal punishment must eventually punish people is not true. A system which admits only the most impartial of evidence and operates for only a finite period of time will not necessarily punish any innocent individual. This refutation, however, merely weakens Schedler's argument. For the great majority of systems, which are not set up in this manner, his argument would still be valid.

Schedler also incorrectly ignored the distinction between intention and knowledge of punishment of innocent people. It is true that many retributivists object to telishment simply because it results in the inflicting of punishment upon innocent parties. However, other retributivists, Kant among them, discuss the motivation behind the inflicting of telishment. Schedler's argument is valid only for the former group, since legal punishment is not implemented with the intention of punishing any innocent person.

Neither of these refutations have succeeded in rendering Schedler's argument entirely invalid. The more fundamental problem with Schedler's argument lies in his viewing legal punishment and telishment as systems rather than as particular instances. The retributivist's supporting a system that he knows will eventually punish an innocent person is entirely beside the point. The system is nothing more than the sum of many particular instances of punishment, and in each particular instance, the official believes that he is punishing a guilty party. On the other hand, every particular case of telishment is implemented with the knowledge that an innocent party will suffer. It is the particular case of telishment that the retributivist condemns, and the particular instance of legal punishment which he advocates.

It was not the purpose of this essay to deny the possibility of a retributivist coming to the decision that he cannot tolerate legal punishment. Rather I have demonstrated that Schedler's argument, as a proof that the retributivist cannot consistently support legal punishment while condemning telishment, fails.

(Name Withheld)

The Benefits of Humanistic Approaches to the Study of the Law

Much criticism recently appeared in popular periodicals concerning the "criminal" way law is taught in schools. Oddly enough, this criticism makes me all the more attracted to a legal education. For at least one effect of this criticism is a more humanistic approach to the study of law. This change benefits not only legal studies, but the humanities, and possibly even modern culture itself.

Most forms of modern humanism assume a world that is inherently senseless. The humanist's task is not to find meaning in an external, objective reality but to impose meaning on what is otherwise chaos and inhuman homelessness (*unheimlichkeit*). The problem with the humanist's program is that the humanist himself, as the acknowledged legislator of the world, has no authority. His values and meanings are his own creation and thus mere fictions; he cannot escape his assumption of an absurd world.

Humanistic approaches to the study of the law provide a means of grounding humanistic values. Legal institutions are at the center of American culture; they reflect and, to some extent, foster values. Because of this institutional anchor, humanistic legal studies give authority and credibility to humanistic values. These values become not mere fictions, but institutional realities.

The study of law thus enables humanists to reinstitute their meanings and values in a culture very badly in need of them. And in turn, humanistic approaches give legal studies a richer and more interesting context.

Craig Coben

One often hears that fluency in foreign languages has many practical purposes and opens new career possibilities. Indeed, language proficiency is a useful skill in international trade, finance, law and diplomacy. For me, however, foreign tongues also represent the best of a liberal arts education: languages enhance my ability to understand what other people do, create and articulate. If one of the primary goals of a liberal arts education is to liberate students so that they may have choices in the shaping of their lives and in defining the needs of society as citizens, the study of foreign languages will contribute to this objective. Languages expand the freedom of a student, exposing him or her to different modes of thought and widening his or her horizon of civilization. Foreign languages have consequently always interested me, and I have devoted much time to learning them well. I speak Spanish and Italian very fluently and French reasonably well, and this year I am studying Swahili.

The shock of recognition in any intellectual field is intensely gratifying, and comprehending a text written in a foreign language produces an extraordinary feeling of accomplishment. Listening to the unmediated voices of Cervantes, Calvino, or Stendahl speaking from the fundaments of human experience, I experience pleasures of understanding for which there is no substitute elsewhere. Reading the actual accounts of the first Spanish *cronistas* (chroniclers) of the New World and their attempts to come to grips with what to them was a completely alien culture, I sense a special immediacy to the Conquest of America. The original text stimulates my historical imagination about words and events that makes them much more interesting. When I grasp the wit of a pun or the subtle irony of a literary passage in a foreign language, I realize the inherent inadequacy of translation, no matter how skillfully the English version may have been rendered; I also experience the delightful feeling that I know the language not as just a series of symbols to be translated awkwardly into English, but as a living medium of communication endowed with its own ways of explaining the world. Furthermore, looking at a text in a language I do not know, I still try to decipher its meaning; the text seems almost a sacred arcanum whose holy mysteries are wrapped in words and symbols I cannot understand. I feel impelled to find my way into the obscure text. These struggles for understanding human expressions of many kinds and for making a foreign language less "foreign" leave an indelible mark on my sensibility.

The words of foreign languages reveal something about the psychology and culture of a people and thus provide me with a different perspective of life. My recent five-month odyssey through Southern Mexico and Guatemala underscored the importance of foreign language acquisition. A religious festival I witnessed last spring in the jungle village of Tenejapa, Mexico, would have seemed merely a quaint indigenous ceremony, if a gentleman there had not explained to me in Spanish the sacred meaning of the dances and apparel of the procession leaders. Tenejapa is an isolated hamlet attracting few Western travellers, and a good knowledge of Spanish (or the local Mayan dialect) furnishes the chance to unearth a few nuggets about the world-view of the Tenejapan Indians of Southern Mexico.

Unfortunately, Americans have the dubious but probably deserved reputation of generally refusing to learn foreign languages. This monolingualism often reflects an ignorance or even disdain of foreign cultures. In the increased interdependence of the modern world, this incapacity to understand people of other cultures is often embarassing and sometimes dangerous to the national welfare. Such a peculiarly pre-Copernican focus—the ethnocentrist sees his or her own culture as the spiritual center around which the rest of the world revolves—spawns suspicion and mistrust between different ethnic groups and nationalities. I immerse myself in foreign languages, literatures and cultures to combat a crude world devoid of understanding. As a group Tour Director in Spain and France, I tried not only to find lost luggage at hectic airports, but also to convince my American clients that other people have very good reasons to be proud of their idioms, ethnic heritages, and distinct traditions. I hope that, when they think of Spain, some clients will remember not just such touristy goodies as Lladro porcelain and Majorica pearls, but also the architectural splendor of the Alhambra of Granda and the reasons for the triple character—*alcazaba* (fortress), *alcazar* (palace) and *medina* (city)—for this Moorish complex.

Foreign languages require much time and patience to learn, and speaking another tongue often produces feelings of uneasiness in the beginning. Nevertheless, the benefits of understanding other people and of communicating with them reward those efforts. Learning a foreign language expands one's vision prodigiously into a whole new realm of human understanding. Foreign language acquisition is necessary to be an educated, sentient person with empathy for foreign peoples and cultures and a capacity to experience the world through other eyes and other words. By helping me understand other people, languages help me understand myself and thus sustain my continuous endeavor to discover what is worth learning and doing.

James Tourtelott

In answer to the instruction to "Write an essay on the subject of your choice, not to exceed 250 words" —

As a man who has earned his living by designing essay questions and reading semi-literate responses to them, I have some sympathy for the beleaguered members of admissions committees who have to slash their way through forests of dangling participles. As a man who spends more time providing writing samples than he expected to at his age, I have also become fascinated by the forms which requests for such samples take.

There are two fundamental varieties of such essay questions—the inordinately detailed and the deliberately vague. The one example of the inordinately detailed essay question with which every applicant to law school is acquainted is the LSAT writing sample, the setting forth of which is as jammed with unnecessary information as a Jimmy Carter press conference. There is of course a reason, or at least an excuse, for this. The details are meant to furnish a basis for argument. Why one cannot trust a group of reasonably intelligent folks to dream up a line of argument I do not know, but perhaps there is wisdom in not encouraging people who plan to practice law to embroider on reality.

If the LSAT writing sample question is elaborate, the question I am answering is more streamlined. The advantage of this form is immediately evident: the English major can recycle his old Byron notes instead of trying to explain Marbury versus Madison; the poli. sci. student can expatiate on Gramm-Rudman instead of manufacturing acceptable reasons why he wants to study law—the prospect of a Mercedes not being the sort of thing one can mention in such circumstances. There are of course dangers for the respondent to such a question: the impassioned defense of the chair as deterrent may be read by a board member of the Civil Liberties Union, the exegesis of Bruce Springsteen by a man who thinks Beethoven a Bolshevik. But since it is the examiner's duty to cast aside prejudice, this is a minor problem.

The mangling of the English language, however, is not a minor problem. That in which one is interested is the "object," not the "subject" of one's interests. One can of course be interested in a subject—water polo, the paintings of Vermeer, grammar. That is "a subject which interests" one. If you want to say, "Write about a subject which interests you," say it. In the next edition of this application, for choice.

Injustice Witnessed:
Essays About Crimes of All Sorts

In a utopian world, there would be no need for law—or lawyers. The law student's true *raison d'etre* is the existence of injustice. The desire to fix that is the purest of motivations for the aspiring lawyer.

You may see injustice in a more abstract, political form, as Stephanie Cotsirlilos did, or you may even play a role yourself, as Steven Lofchie found himself doing. Both of these pieces are especially powerful, because rather than talking with pretentious adjectives about motivations, they recreate scenes that thrust the reader into their experience.

In writing an essay like these, you can demonstrate your sensitivity to the world's imperfections and your sympathy to troubles which may not be your own. You show that you can be trusted to treat your law degree—and the knowledge it represents—as more than a money machine.

Stephanie Cotsirilos

Epidaurus, Circa 1970

My mother and I arrived at the hills of Epidaurus in the early evening and walked up the old path to the theatre. Distant relatives lay in the countryside, their bones becoming part of the rock formation below the olive trees and the sand. We found our places in the stone amphitheatre, which broke at its edges into boulders. We had come to see Euripides' *Electra*. My mother crumpled a kleenex, and the acoustics made it sound like a small hurricane in her hand.

The military junta was still in power in Greece that summer. In Athens, we had dined with a Greek couple, both liberal academics who loved to dance. The wife had become increasingly nervous as her husband made jokes about the government within earshot of the waiters. Years later, in New York, a young woman would relate to me her experience of the penalty this wife feared for her husband.

Now, at Epidaurus, junta elite entered the theatre. We watched the audience stand and applaud briefly, as required.

Dusk fell and the play began, repeating its ancient litany of personal betrayal and political struggle. Finally, Electra and Orestes stood silently at opposite ends of the stage; and the actors' moment of recognition spilled beyond the boundaries of the play. The performers' silence communicated, deliberately, defiance and a demand for liberty. So when brother and sister broke and ran into each other's arms, the theatre at Epidaurus exploded with the sound of Greeks on their feet, cheering and applauding around the seated, unsmiling military. This time, my mother and I applauded too. Many minutes passed before the actors would continue the play.

Steven Lofchie

Driving a Cab in New York City

A teen-ager wearing a hooded sweatshirt opened my cab door. He and two friends piled into the back. A fourth man wanted to sit beside me. It was late and my wallet was so stuffed it wouldn't fold. I motioned him into the back. He asked, "You nervous to let me sit with you?" That he must challenge me was a rule of our game. He likely had a knife and might try to rob me if it seemed easy.

My riders gave as their destination the Red Hook projects, a complex of tall, ugly buildings near the elevated tracks in Brooklyn. I drove fast and erratically, throwing them about the back seat, keeping them uncomfortable. I watched them in the rear view mirror. Their conversation was too low for me to hear. We sped and jolted past the gutted buildings and the garbage-piled lots.

At our destination, I slammed both the gas and brake. Then I shifted into reverse. When the rear door opened, I released the brake. The cab raced backward. This was one of my standard defenses. "No one leaves before paying," I announced.

Crumpled money was pushed through the partition. Two riders burst out. I wouldn't let them near my window. The cab rolled forward and gained speed, two passengers caught inside. One banged his fist behind my head. The partition clattered. I slowed to twenty, slow enough for them to jump. One stumbled clumsily.

For six years, mostly part-time, I drove cabs. The job was a succession of threatening situations. When I was sufficiently careful, I did not learn if the threats had been real or imagined.

(Name Withheld)

Michael Stewart was an inner-city "kid" who kept to himself, his mother remembers. He fancied himself an artist, and to this end, he drew subway art, even though this was illegal. One day while he was creating this outlawed form of expression, he was arrested by a policeman. From this point on the details as to what happened are somewhat obscure. What is known is that the would-be Picasso ended up in a coma with cuts and bruises all over his body. Two weeks later, Mrs. Stewart laid to rest her nineteen year old son.

There were several eyewitnesses to the events of the afternoon on which Michael Stewart was mortally wounded. Though the stories varied according to how much each person saw, the one constant thread in each was that he was beaten by policemen. Not just one or two policemen, but *ten* officers took part in "subduing" Stewart. "New York's Finest", explained their actions as necessary in controlling the suspect. They only used their nightsticks while it was necessary, afterwhich they brought Stewart to jail. However, the same eyewitnesses concur that Stewart was in no way resisting the policemen. They beat him unmercifully in broad daylight, and his only real "crime" was being black in a white man's world.

The New York City District Attorney's office immediately and inexplicably cleared seven of the officers of any wrong doing. The other three officers were ordered to stand trial. They were eventually found not guilty, after the coroner changed his story about the autopsy on three different occasions. Michael Stewart's death was ruled a suicide, although the evidence proved that he could not have beat himself into a coma.

This is an example of the brand of justice that black Americans have come to expect. A jury of our peers, still means a jury of our "overseers". The problem will only be righted by black people because it is for black people. Yet, black lawyers would rather go on to the large law firm which will pay him/her the "big money". This is the dilemma that will face me in a few short years. Sometimes I think that I cannot make a difference all by myself. But by becoming part of the system that condones and supports this kind of justice, I would be a part of the problem. I pray to God that I find a solution that I can live with, and still live with myself.

(Name Withheld)

When I was twelve years old, I wanted to be the first woman president of the United States. Throughout high school, I prepared for this vocation; majoring in political science in college was an easy choice. Much to my surprise, though, political science led me to change my plans and abandon the race for the White House.

Elective office cannot be part of the American dream for everyone. Expensive political technologies such as media advertising and consulting make large campaign coffers necessary for competitive candidates. Moreover, because of money's role in elections, contributors have special access to politics and can exercise disproportionate influence in the decision-making process.

Summer experiences verified these conclusions. While an intern at Common Cause, a citizens' lobby group specializing in campaign finance, I saw that political action committees and wealthy contributors play a large role in the decision-making process. Subsequent internships with Senators John Heinz, the chairman of the Republican Senatorial Campaign Committee, and Arlen Specter, a Republican incumbent seeking reelection in 1986, evidenced how legislators frequently plan their strategies in an effort to appease monied interests.

Running for office has lost its appeal. Rather than destroying my dreams, though, disillusionment has pointed me in a new direction and has increased my desire to work towards electoral reform. Law school may tarnish more of my golden ideals. However, I have learned to look beyond my disappointments and look forward to the challenges that accompany them.

L. Roger Boord

The law is rooted in history and philosophy. To fully understand the law, each person must make his own journey through those subjects and arrive at his own perceptions. In 1987, I attended the University of Cambridge, England, where I studied modern political thought and the history of World War II. The purpose of this essay is to show how my studies and my experiences traveling influenced my desire to work for human rights through the legal profession.

Amsterdam, The Netherlands. In a room hidden in the back of an office building on the Prisengracht Canal, I saw pasted on the walls a collection of pictures of Hollywood movie stars and European figures taken from magazines of the 1940's. This, and the scattered papers of a diary, were the only surviving remnants found of a young Jewish girl who had hidden in this secret annex until deported to Bergen-Belsen in 1944.

Even after forty years, the atrocities committed by the Nazi regime shock the civilized mind. The photographs of piles of mutilated corpses leave me in bewildering numbness, but seeing the Anne Frank house personalized the horror by applying a face, a soul to one of those victims. The experience raised the difficult question: Why was life taken from the innocent? I could only find the answer by understanding the process by which innocent life can become valueless.

West Berlin, Federal Republic of Germany. I saw West Berlin today as a bright metropolis reflecting a modern Germany prospering in the confidence of its own success. But the Germany of the young Adolf Hitler was engulfed in political and economic turmoil. The Weimer Republic seemed too burdened with parliamentary weaknesses to deal effectively with economic chaos and the growing threats of Soviet communism.

Hitler offered a radical solution, but few fully comprehended his ominous words: "In the struggle between two philosophies, only can the weapon of brute force, persistently and ruthlessly applied, lead to a decision for the side it supports."

Within four weeks of his rise to Chancellor, Hitler abolished freedom of speech, press, assembly, and the laws against arbitrary search and seizure. This act formed the real basis for Nazi rule since it enabled the police to bypass the courts. As Goering put it, "The law and the will of the Fuhrer are one." Human rights and the rule of law had ceased to exist in Germany.

(East) Berlin, German Democratic Republic. Many Germans saw Hitler as a leader who could protect their nation from the domination of Soviet Communism. But because the Fuhrer put himself above the law, that fear became reality in a separate Germany. East Berlin is the European communist model of happiness and prosperity. To me it was like an amusement park, without amusement. Under the cold, colorless apartment buildings sagging with age and neglect, I saw Soviet soldiers stroll the streets. A colossal statue of Lenin looms ominously in the center of the city, not far from where parallel concrete walls separated by a 200 yard strip of death imprison a nation still deprived of the rule of law. As I surveyed this grim scene I reflected on the similarities in political reality between Hitler's race-socialism and Lenin's class-socialism.

In 1917, Lenin seized power from the Russian Provisional Government. He described his dictatorship as "the rule—unrestricted by law and based on force—of the proletariat over the bourgeoisie." The courts were replaced by revolutionary tribunals and Lenin's secret police. The purpose was to purge the nation of those people whom Lenin classified as "harmful insects"—i.e. to kill people collectively and not individually. As Cheka official M.Y. Latsis explained,

> "We are not carrying out war against individuals. We are exterminating the bourgeoise as a class. We are not looking for evidence or witnesses... The first question we ask is—to what class does he belong, what are his origins, upbringing, education or profession? These questions define the fate of accused."

Munich, F.R.G. Hitler had indeed learned well from Soviet Russia. At the Nazi prison camp Dachau, I saw the grisly results of the aboliton of law—prison cells for the untried, with the crematorium in efficient proximity. I realized that thousands suffered and died because Nazi ideology could not tolerate their living.

Here was the answer to my question—the diabolical process which sets rule of law aside, extinguishing the hopes and dreams of precious individuals like Anne Frank.

> Sometimes it is said that man cannot be trusted with the government of himself. Can he, then, be trusted with the government of others? Let history answer this question.
>
> Thomas Jefferson

Charlottesville, Virginia. I believe that the concepts of liberal democracy and the rule of law are founded first, upon the belief in eternal moral principles which secure "self-evident" and "inalienable" rights to every human being; and secondly, on the philosophy that each individual is responsible for his own behavior, as well as morally obligated to live within the limitations posed by the rights of others. No circumstance of "class struggle," "racial preservation," or any assumed need to go "above the law" can justify abolishing these rights. Human beings can only be properly judged individually, and only through such judgement under the due process of law can a government legitimately take forcible action against any person.

But denial of human rights is still commonplace in 1987. When an enemy is perceived to be at a nation's throat, the tendency is, as Hitler put it, to meet lawlessness with equal lawlessness. But the question is: Can a nation's moral fiber be stretched to whatever shape seems expedient to preserve it?

We must remember that in essence, a nation is what it stands for, especially when standing for that something becomes most difficult. And the "somethings" for which the United States must first stand are justice, truth, and the value of every human being.

I wish to dedicate myself to promotion and protection of these principles. The essence of individual human rights is absolute and universal. That was as clear and essential to a fourteen year-old Dutch girl in 1944 as it is to a twenty-one year old American college student in 1987, or it was to his school's founder in 1776.

> I know what I want, I have a goal, an opinion, I have a religion and love. Let me be myself and then I am satisfied.
>
> Anne Frank

Jugglers:
Essays About Applicants
With Colorful Backgrounds

The variety of scenarios, cases, decisions, people, and ideas lawyers encounter attracts many students to the profession. Most law schools, meanwhile, are looking for a body of diverse students that can stimulate each other and bring a variety of perspectives and experiences to the school.

One successful angle for an essay, then, is to show how much a Renaissance person you are. "A diverse class is a better class," one Dean told us. "If I could have the perfect class, the only thing I can say for sure is that it would have 375 very different people."

Discussing how all of your activities, skills, and accomplishments fit together can show your work ethic, your versatility, and your passion. But no one wants to read a resume. Explain how, for example, your love of music and your Haitian background make you a more vivid, sensitive, driven, and/or exciting person. Interesting and telling detail is the key to effective writing. Show and explain—don't just talk.

Jay Pomerantz describes how teaching, day care, and music have honed his business and legal skills. His resume—which might seem flaky or undirected to a high-powered lawyer—is revealed to be an excellent preparation for law school.

Pomerantz succeeds because he challenges the reader to think about familiar subjects in a new way and because he supports his assertions with concrete examples that are interesting and amusing.

In the next essay, Tyson Branyan avoids what he calls "Lincolnesque" statements, and as a result his piece is more readable and relevant than its length suggests.

Branyan has managed to pull-off the "preemptive" essay. In discussing his career and his background, he addresses potential objections before they can be raised. While he admits that his experiences may not be deep, he argues that a law education offers the chance to become a "specialist." He designated American Indian as his background (though he is only one-eighth Choctaw), but he argues that he "felt" Indian growing up.

Merely by showing that he has *thought* about these shadows, Branyan melts their damage and even turns them to his advantage.

Jay Pomerantz

I have just finished three active and concurrent career explorations. They consist of directing an after-school day care, teaching at the University of California at Santa Cruz, and working as a musican. Each job has challenged my ability to communicate effectively, to think precisely while under pressure, and to organize a large number of details. All require creative decision making. These work experiences have been invaluable; coinciding with the self-exploration of my twenties, they have served as extended and comprehensive aptitude tests. I have pinpointed the kinds of activities I enjoy, and those in which I excel. My personal statement is devoted to outlining these activities, and to discussing how they led me to the conclusion that I should pursue a career in law.

Directing a day care demands the ability to do many things well—almost at once. It is common that in a single five minute period, I have to deal with: (1) two children who have just trashed the school bathroom; (2) another who has just discovered lice in her hair; (3) a boy crying because his teacher confiscated a toy; (4) a parent demanding to review the billing records; (5) a mother on the phone asking me not to allow her ex-boyfriend to pick up her child; (6) an aide who cannot find the right project supplies; and (7) a kid hopping the fence. To survive, I have learned patience, the ability to recall a large number of small but important details, and how to delegate responsibility.

My six years in day care have honed my commucation skills, and have introduced me to the world of business management. Children can be demanding, irrational, cunning, and obstinate in ways that adults often never imagine. While it may seem routine to an outsider, the task of convincing a recalcitrant six-year-old to pick up the Legos he just scattered across the room requires negotiating skills of the highest level. A day does not go by when some complicated compromise is not reached to guarantee that a child will comply with the rules without losing faith. (The concepts of fairness and the organic development of a body of laws are everpresent.) Likewise, daily contact with the parents and guardians of over 90 children has taught me to choose my words with precision and care. As director, I am responsible for an annual budget of over $100,000.00, the hiring, training, and supervision of a staff of five, the purchase of all supplies, and the monthly billing. The fact that the program has more than doubled in size over the last three years has greatly increased the level of these activities. I found that I like managing both people and money; career conversations with attorneys have confirmed that these skills figure prominently in the practice of law.

Music is an enduring and compelling interest. Business skills have enabled me to translate that interest into a wide range of musical activity. I have successfully enlisted the support of professional studios in the recording of my own material, resulting in a full-length album that I co-produced, packaged, and distributed. Club owners and booking agents are some of the most irascible people on the planet, but I have learned to deal with them effectively. My band performs regularly at local clubs. A publishing company offered me a contract for several songs. An eye-opening meeting with a music lawyer in Monterey demonstrated the complexity of entering into such agreements. It also demonstrated the potential for combining music and law in a legal career. I strongly believe that different careers and interests can be integrated; they need not be mutually exclusive. I intend to practice law with this in mind.

It was my involvement with music that sparked a passion for all the arts. My undergraduate degree in Art History led directly to an appointment as a university teaching assistant. This, in turn, resulted in my current job as Visiting Lecturer at the University of California at Santa Cruz. This fall marks the fourth year that I have been one of the instructors for the Core Course, an interdisciplinary class for first year students. The course uses the study of the arts to introduce the students to new modes of thinking and writing. Small tutorials are the primary teaching unit. I have planned and led these tutorials, given lectures on a wide range of topics, written all my course assignments, commented on student essays, and written the Student Narrative Evaluations.

Frankly, I feel that I have learned all I can as day care director *cum* university teacher. Life and lessons in both arenas are recycling. I am now thirty. My cognitive self demands new direction and a longer-range sense of purpose. It is this voice that has lobbied for the examination of law as a career.

To this end, I made a set of systematic career investigations. First, I consulted with the law advisor at UC Santa Cruz. Next, I arranged a half dozen interviews with practicing attorneys. These interviews left me with a detailed, unidealized notion of what it means to work as an attorney; they supported my assumption that what I have learned since graduation will serve me well in the field. And finally, I attended a number of law classes. My interest in the material confirmed my decision to attend law school. Any concern I had about making the jump into this competitive field, with its fair share of difficult people, evaporated when one of my lawyer/day care parents refused to switch jobs with me for the day—he feared he could not handle the intensity of the day care.

In the introduction to the Standard application, the notion that a lawyer must confront a diverse set of challenges is stressed. I have enclosed the tape album I co-wrote and produced as evidence of my ability to do just that. The making of this tape required the necessary music and organizational skills, a fluency in computer language in the application of MIDI and SMPTE, graphics and advertising skills, as well as the overriding ability to make decisions, to solve problems, and to see something through to its completion.

Tyson Branyan

If the Committee has waded through my academic/work history, it should be clear that I've done a great many different things. To keep that history to a manageable length, I've left out many details as to responsibilities and items learned along the way. You will just have to read between the lines and accept that much useful knowledge was acquired and useful skills honed. I didn't even discuss avocational areas, such as the weekends I spent roadracing motorcycles at tracks all over California or the fact that my job enabled me to pilot a small plane over most of the western United States. I've done geological work in Alaska and have traveled extensively in Europe and Great Britain. I'm still a competitive athlete and often coach youth sports. I've worked very hard, but I've also had some fun. I've enjoyed my work and the small financial rewards it has brought with it.

There is one thing however, that I have not enjoyed. That is that I've always been a generalist. The Committee can deduce this. I went from Geol/Engnr to Soc/Anthro and back again. I've done a wide variety of jobs, each with wide responsibilities. Though a partner in TYDECO, I've basically been self-employed these past four years. It suits me well and keeps me sharp to have this variety, but it is difficult to be continually climbing the learning curve. There are no classes offered anywhere entitled "Uranium Exploration 101" or "How to Get a Good Deal from Major Oil Companies". I'm basically self-taught in the "South Texas School of Hard Knocks", and in most cases this has been more than adequate, if expensive at times.

However, self-taught has no place in the world of laws. I've had to constantly defer to others as to technicalities and implications of rules, regulations, contracts and agency jurisdictions. I've had both good and bad experiences with retained counsel throughout the years. In the back of my mind though, there always ran two strains of emotion: first a feeling of being at a disadvantage because of my ignorance, and second, a little jealousy that this person was dealing with very interesting issues that I liked and for which I had a good feel. Last year the final straw came when I was involved with the purchase of a tungsten mill in Nederland, Colorado. By the time we had wrangled through the legal complexities of an 1880's water right, centered in the Denver watershed, I knew my future lay in a career in law.

The experience with the water right convinced me that I would enjoy and succeed in a career in law, and that I should pursue this long postponed goal. Without much guidance, I found out how to register with LSDAS and took the LSAT this past December. My score of 41 is not stunning, but will insure that I have a good chance to be accepted at the schools to which I've applied here in the Southwest.

Frankly, I never considered applying to Cornell until February 1st. It was then that I received the letter from Dean Geiger which is sent to certain LSDAS Referral Service Candidates. In this letter he outlined some of Cornell's assets and just importantly, waived the February 1st application deadline for recepients of that letter. Because of this correspondence I was motivated to speak to friends and others who are familiar with your institution and with Ithaca. I also spoke with your admissions office, a recent Cornell Law graduate and with Mr. Chris Stearns (Navajo), your American Indian Law students' representative. I wanted to be sure that Cornell was truly interested in a diverse student population.

Mr. Stearns and I discussed many aspects of my background and how it related to the admissions process at Cornell. Evidently, I received the Dean's letter because I had marked that I was Native American when registering with LSDAS. I related that I am "only" an eighth or sixteenth Choctaw by blood and, because it is so patently self-serving, I have very mixed feelings about even mentioning it during the admissions process. In no way have I ever been disadvantaged due to my Choctaw heritage. On the other hand, after a lifetime of being proud of this heritage and being especially close to my Grandmother Nona, I wasn't about to deny it now. It aggravates me to discuss (defend?) my "Indianness" as I'm doing here, but Mr. Stearns and others assured me that your admissions committee would be interested in hearing some of what I related to him.

My grandmother was born Nona Mae Collins at the turn of the century in Indian Territory. For governmental purposes she was classified as ¼ Choctaw. She lived in a small settlement named Ti, I.T., and was later sent to the Choctaw boarding schools for girls in Tuskahoma. Typically, speaking Choctaw was forbidden here, as assimilation was the order of the day. In most respects, assimilation worked well for her, as it did for most individual Choctaws. She got a job in the Oklahoma City stockyards, married a cowboy and had three daughters. Two of these daughters married Indian; my mother did not. It was a shock to me to finally realize that I was "less Indian" than my cousins, but nonetheless, we were all equally part of a grand matrilineal family, dominated by one very special Choctaw woman; a woman who entertained us with her stories and invigorated us with her love. Today Nona is an old, frail, yet still elegant woman who is pleased with her life and her family.

There's more that I could say about all of this; but I'm not, because my homelife was what I considered normal middle class. I grew up in Cushing, Oklahoma, a town of 6,500 that I mistakenly thought was a city. I was in high school when my family moved to Southern California, and I quickly learned that Cushing wasn't much of a place. I was at no disadvantage though and did well in California schools and graduated from Chapman College with honors. As my work history shows, I've had success in business and life in general. I'm happily married and now have two children, age 4 and 2.

I've written my life story in this statement partly to respond to Item No. 6 on your admissions application and also because Cornell seems genuinely interested in the total candidate. I've applied to several other schools to which my statements could only be described as "terse", because I feel my resume, my academic career and my LSAT scores can speak for themselves. I'm sure I would not have written this much for Cornell if I had applied prior to February 1st and had I not received Dean Geiger's letter. This despite being advised that Ivy League schools particularly like statements that are "Lincolnesque".

I've resisted this while trying to just sketch in the facts.

I would like to attend Cornell because of what I now believe I know about it. The school turns out competent people who are not limited as to where or what they can practice. It is evidently challenging and interesting, and I'd be disappointed if Cornell wasn't difficult. Importantly, Ithaca seems like a place my family would find comfortable for a few years. Cornell also offers a chance to study Indian law and that is one of my personal measures for an acceptable law school. Though I am only going to attend a school that offers this possibility, what I'll do with it I refuse to speculate. The Indians I know are like anybody else, they need competent counsel for rather ordinary situations. If Cornell wants students with certain backgrounds in order to round out its official ethnic population, I'm not sure I'm the candidate for you. If the slot I am seeking is reserved only for disadvantaged Indian students it would be a disservice to several parties to offer it to me. On the other hand, If Cornell truly wants people who have diverse backgrounds and who will be a credit to the University after graduation, I do feel I have the qualifications for which you are looking and believe my attendance at Cornell might work out well for all of us.

(Name Withheld)

During the previous four years I have been employed as Principal at a high school in Illinois. The school was a boarding school for students gifted in dance and/or music. My duties included the coordination of all programs offered; presentations to the board of directors; development, supervision, and evaluation of all academic faculty; course and curriculum development; student advisement and placement; implememtation of the budget; designing master schedules for faculty and students; development of all school handbooks; and supervision of all extra-curricular organizations and student activities.

Before coming to the school, I was employed as a Social Studies Teacher at a junior high school. I was responsible for developing the curriculum as well as working on the budget and ordering materials. I also served as Assistant Gifted Coordinator; assisted the Student Council; served as a member of the parent/teacher committee; coached track; and was responsible for a variety of after-school activities involving students from grades K through 8.

I have been successful in a variety of situations dealing with diverse groups of people. I was responsible for managing a family-owned grocery store in Illinois. I worked with various minorities as a Youth Supervisor in the Illinois area. I taught many Amish students during my stay in Arcola and I was associated with world-renowned artists as well as an international student body at my high school. I believe these successful experiences illustrate that I possess the interpersonal skills as well as the integrity, energy, and determination required by a career in law.

I believe that my membership in Kappa Delta Pi and Phi Delta Kappa along with my success in graduate school to be a more accurate reflection of my academic potential than my undergraduate work. I am eager and anxious to apply my academic and professional experiences at the Indiana University School of Law and I am confident that my addition to the student body would be a positive and productive one for both myself and the School.

(Name Withheld)

A career in law is often portrayed by the media as glamorous; it is viewed as prestigious, powerful, and financially rewarding. As a prospective law student, these items appeal to me; but I also realize that a legal career will involve strenuous pressures, exacting challenges, unrelenting hard work, and careful attention to detail.

The interests and talents that I have are diverse, and this diversity will be an advantage for me in law school as well as in a legal career. My interests and achievements, both academic and personal, are well balanced. My college major, mathematics, is a discipline requiring skills in logic and analysis that will be invaluable in my study of law. My minor was in English with emphases in composition, research, and communications. The excellent grades I have earned in mathematics and English reflect my ability to think clearly and logically as well as my proficiency in communicating those thoughts effectively. I have also excelled in all other academic areas outside my major fields of study that portend an aptitude for success in law, such as in public speaking or debate. Furthermore, my personal experiences reflect a diversity of interests and strengths. Through active involvement in church ministries and varied work experiences, I have had the opportunity to deal with people from all backgrounds. This involvement has helped me to further develop a good rapport with people and a healthy social consciousness. A career in law would be ideal for allowing me to use and develop all of these talents, interests, and experiences.

I look forward to the exciting challenges a career in law will offer. A highly self-motivated, goal-oriented hard worker, I am very competitive by nature, but also strive for quality and excellence when working independently or at a team effort. With a strong personal commitment to integrity, I make every effort to achieve and excel in even the most stressful circumstances and environments.

Because of my diversity of interests and abilities, and my ethics of hard work and integrity, I believe I would be an outstanding student at Indiana and a successful attorney. In all I do, I strive for excellence; and to be accepted by Indiana University School of Law, with its history of excellence, would be an honor.

(Name Withheld)

One may ask, "Why would a psychology major be interested in a legal career?". Of all the questions that have been broached concerning my plans to enter law school, this one most frequently occurs. In my opinion there are natural links between law and psychology due to the fact that they are both human services. My interest in human problems and interpersonal communication which led me to pursue psychology, now motivates my pursuit of law. Law epitimizes these attractions in psychology as well as encourages analytical thought processes, rational problem solving, and defining a concrete legal methodolgy for solutions.

Law began to seriously interest me last year while I was working as an adolescent counselor in a psychiatric hospital. In daily counseling situations I was given opportunity to utilize my listening, analytical, and rational skills. I learned that active listening to both the words verbalized and the feelings left submerged was difficult. A vital component of successful treatment, I realized, was interpersonal communication. In counseling situations I also incorporated both analytical and rational thought processes to develop a diagnosis of the patient's problem. Interacting with people in this manner truly challenged me while solidifying my determination to enter a people-helping profession.

Psychology helps people deal with their mental and emotional problems. After considering not only my desire to help people but also my interpersonal and analytical apptitudes I concluded that my desire is to serve people in a more comprehensive way. Law serves as an umbrella under which problems ranging from corporate disagreements to personal claims are resolved. Although I desire to utilize the interpersonal skills gained by my training in psychology, I am also attracted by the analytical aspects of law. Inherent within law are opportunities to exercise my altruistic characteristics and satisfy my desire to develop definite analytical solutions. I believe my proficiency in psychology enhanced by my personal experiences enables me to enter the field of law with unique advantages.

About the Author

Boykin Curry, a New Jersey native, graduated from Yale in 1988. He and Yale classmate Brian Kasbar created the *Essays That Worked* series in 1986. *Essays That Worked—For Law Schools* is the third book in the series, which has sold over 100,000 copies and has received high praise from the media and admissions officers nationwide. Curry plans to pursue a career in business and continue to develop entrepreneurial projects.

More Great Books
from Mustang Publishing

Europe for Free by Brian Butler. If you think a trip to Europe is just one long exercise in cashing traveler's checks, then this is the book for you. The author describes *thousands* of activities, sights, and other fun things to see and do—and nothing costs one single lira, franc, or pfennig. *"A valuable resource"—U.P.I.* **$9.95**

Europe: Where the Fun Is by Rollin Riggs & Bruce Jacobsen. No hotels, no museums, no historic sights. Just the wildest bars, the coolest nightclubs, the hottest beaches, the weirdest flea markets—just the fun stuff, in all the major cities of Europe. A terrific supplement to the major guidebooks. *Named one of the 25 best European travel guides by "Changing Times" magazine.* **$8.95**

Hawaii for Free by Frances Carter. How could anyone improve on Hawaii, America's paradise? Simple. Make a vacation there a whole lot cheaper! From free pineapple to free campsites, this book describes hundreds of free things to do and see all over Hawaii—and nothing costs a penny. *"Invaluable"—Aloha Magazine.* **$7.95**

Essays That Worked: 50 Essays from Successful Applications to the Nation's Top Colleges by Boykin Curry & Brian Kasbar. Applying to college? Dread the essay? This book can help. With 50 outstanding essays from schools like Yale, Duke, and Wesleyan—plus lots of helpful advice from admissions officers—this book will inspire any college applicant. *"50 admissions essays, each one a winner"—New York Times.* **$8.95**

Essays That Worked—For Business Schools by Boykin Curry & Brian Kasbar. With graduates from top MBA programs waltzing into jobs paying $70,000 a year, it's no wonder that the competition to top business schools is so fierce. With 35 excellent essays from B-schools like Harvard, Yale, and Columbia—plus lots of great advice from admissions officers—this book can give applicants a competitive edge. *"Highly recommended"—Campus USA.* **$8.95**

The Student's Guide to the Best Summer Jobs in Alaska by Josh Groves. Thousands of young adults head for Alaska each summer, seeking jobs in the potentially lucrative fishing industry. This book offers the most thorough information on the Alaska summer job scene available. *"Highly recommended"—The Tartan, Carnegie-Mellon Univ.* **$7.95**

The Complete Book of Beer Drinking Games by Andy Griscom, Ben Rand, & Scott Johnston. Attention party animals! With 50 of the world's greatest beer games—plus lots of "really important stuff"—this book has quickly become the imbiber's bible. Over 150,000 copies sold! *"A classic in American Literature"—The Torch, St. John's Univ.* **$5.95**

Beer Games II: The Exploitative Sequel by Griscom, Rand, Johnston, & Balay. This uproarious sequel is even funnier than the original! With 30 new beer games, more hilarious articles and cartoons, and the wild Beer Catalog, this book must be seen to be believed. *"Absolutely fantastic!"—34th Street Newspaper, Univ. of Pennsylvania.* **$5.95**

Prove It All Night! The Bruce Springsteen Trivia Book by Deborah Mayer. So you think you're an expert on The Boss, eh? Well, then, answer this: Where are 10th Avenue and E Street? Whom did Bruce write *Fire* for? What Bruce songs mention the word "beer"? For the answers, you need this highly entertaining book. A great gift! *"The ultimate '80s quiz"—Associated Press.* **$5.95**

The Cathouses of Nevada: A Sensual Guide by J. R. Schwartz. Over two million people visit the legal brothels of Nevada each year, and this book has become a must for the adventurous traveller. An opinionated, entertaining travel book. Don't go to Nevada without it! *"An essential guide"—Adam Magazine.* **$6.95**

The Survival Game® **: Paintball Strategies & Tactics** by Bill Barnes. Every weekend, thousands of Americans don army fatigues and goggles and head for the woods to play America's fastest growing sport, The Survival Game® (aka "Paintball"). Written for the intermediate and advanced player, this book gives dozens of strategy ideas and tactical tips that will prove invaluable to players and teams. *Available February, 1989.* **$8.95**

———————————

Mustang books should be available at your local bookstore. If not, you may order directly from us. Send a check or money order for the price of the book—plus $1.50 for postage *per book* —to Mustang Publishing, P. O. Box 9327, New Haven, CT 06533. Allow three weeks for delivery.

Add $3.50 per book for delivery in one week. Connecticut residents must add 7.5% sales tax. Foreign orders: U.S. funds only, please, and add $3.00 postage per book ($5.00 for Air Mail).

For a free catalog of Mustang books, send a stamped, self-addressed, business-size envelope to Catalog Request, Mustang Publishing, P. O. Box 9327, New Haven, CT 06533.